D0189272

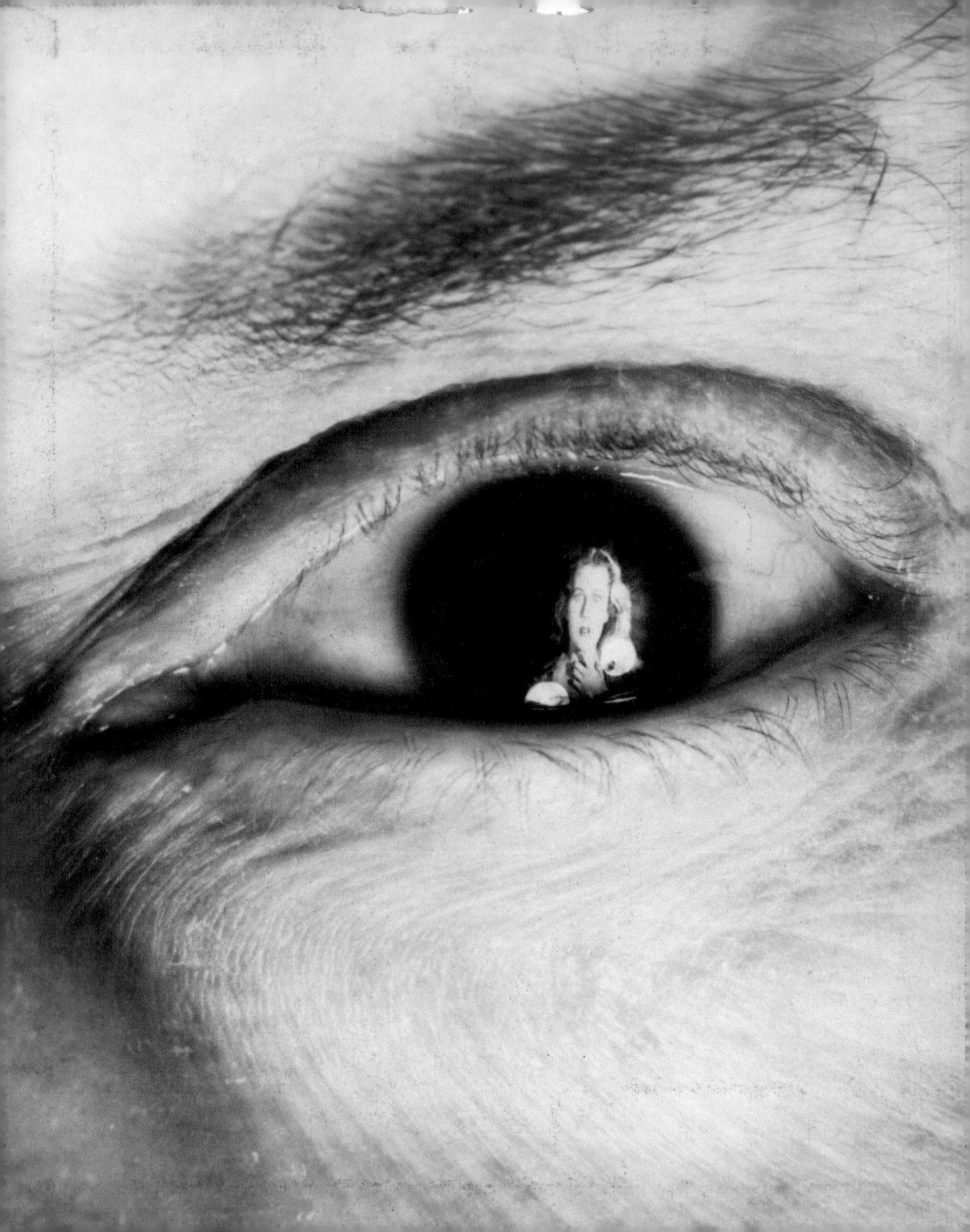

Alain Silver & James Ursini
Paul Duncan (Ed.)

FILM NOIR

TASCHEN

HONGKONG KÖLN LONDON LOS ANGELES MADRID PARIS TOKYO

FRONT & BACK COVER
Publicity still for 'Night of the Hunter' (1955)
Robert Mitchum plays a schizophrenic preacher whose tattooed hands do a lot of smiting.

FIRST PAGE
Still from 'The Sniper' (1952)
After shooting women from rooftops, the alienated and mentally disturbed Eddie Miller (Arthur Franz) releases a tear of relief when the police come to stop him.

FRONTISPIECE
Publicity still for 'The Spiral Staircase' (1946)
The killer, who thinks that "there is no room in the whole world for imperfection," sets his sights on his next victim.

THIS PAGE
1 **Still from 'Murder, My Sweet' (1944)** Philip Marlowe (Dick Powell) meets femme fatale Velma/Mrs Grayle (Claire Trevor).

2 **Still from 'Laura' (1944)** Mark McPherson (Dana Andrews) interrogates the woman he is obsessed with: Laura Hunt (Gene Tierney).

OPPOSITE
1 **Still from 'High Sierra' (1941)** Career criminal Roy 'Mad Dog' Earle (Humphrey Bogart) examines Marie (Ida Lupino), whom he will come to love and respect.
2 **Still from 'The Third Man' (1949)** Enigmatic and elusive Harry Lime (Orson Welles) is hunted down in Vienna's sewers.

PAGES 6/7
On the set of 'Crossroads' (1942)
David Talbot (William Powell) is blackmailed with a past he cannot remember at this atmospheric reproduction of the Pont Neuf in Paris. With a restricted budget and audience during World War Two, cinematographers had to make the most of a few planks of wood, some lights and a fog machine.

To stay informed about upcoming TASCHEN titles, please request our magazine at www.taschen.com/magazine or write to TASCHEN America, 6671 Sunset Boulevard, Suite 1508, USA-Los Angeles, CA 90028, contact-us@taschen.com, Fax: +1-323-463.4442. We will be happy to send you a free copy of our magazine which is filled with information about all of our books.

© 2004 TASCHEN GmbH
Hohenzollernring 53, D–50672 Köln
www.taschen.com
Editor/Layout: Paul Duncan/Wordsmith Solutions
Editorial Coordination: Thierry Nebois, Cologne
Typeface Design: Sense/Net, Andy Disl, Cologne

Printed in China
ISBN-13: 978-3-8228-2261-6
ISBN-10: 3-8228-2261-2

What is 'Noir'?

How did a cycle of the American cinema become one of the most influential movements in film history? During its classic period, which lasted from 1941 to 1958, noir films were derided by critics of the time. Lloyd Shearer, for example, writing a Sunday supplement piece for *The New York Times* ('Crime Certainly Does Pay,' 5 August 1945) mocked the trends in 'crime films' that were 'homicidal,' 'lusty' and filled with 'gut-and-gore crime.' In fact the top echelon of the major studios – Paramount, Twentieth Century-Fox, MGM and Warner Bros. – usually relegated their 'crime films' to B-units and released them on the bottom half of double bills. The other majors – RKO, Universal, United Artists and Columbia – along with poverty-row companies like Producers Releasing Corporation (PRC), pumped them out shamelessly. There were, of course, prestigious exceptions, Academy Award nominees like *The Maltese Falcon* (1941, Warner Bros.), *Laura* (1944, Twentieth Century-Fox) and *Double Indemnity* (1944, Paramount); but even mainstream honours did not save these films from widespread disparagement by the critical community. In fact Shearer's main target in his article is *Double Indemnity*.

How then, with such critical opprobrium heaped upon them and such industry disdain for their market value, did they become valorised as 'film noir'? How did they become a major influence on two subsequent generations of film-makers, including but not limited to Roman Polanski, Francis Ford Coppola, François Truffaut, Martin Scorsese, Claude Chabrol, Lawrence Kasdan, Luc Besson, Quentin Tarantino, Takeshi Kitano, David Fincher, Bertrand Tavernier, Stephen Frears, Spike Lee, Bryan Singer and Neil Jordan? Why, in fact, has this movement, called 'neo-noir', carried on unabated for over three decades? A term coined by Todd Erickson and first discussed at length in the second edition of *Film Noir, An Encyclopedic Reference to the American Style* (1987), neo-noir began with films like Polanski's *Chinatown* (1974), Coppola's *The Conversation* (1974), Scorsese's *Taxi Driver* (1976) and Kasdan's *Body Heat* (1981). It continues up to the present through films like Jordan's *Mona Lisa* (1986), Tarantino's *Reservoir Dogs* (1992) and *Pulp Fiction* (1994), Fincher's *Seven* (1995), Singer's *The Usual Suspects* (1995) and Frears' *The Grifters* (1990) and *Dirty Pretty Things* (2003). Why have the actual French words 'film noir' been incorporated into modern English dictionaries and become part of the lexicon of any self-respecting young film-maker?

Publicity still for 'High Sierra' (1941)
Humphrey Bogart's portrayal of Roy Earle as a bad man yearning for a better life helped to define Bogart's tough guy persona, and is the dividing line between the 1930s Warner Bros. gangster films and the 1940s film noirs.

"An extraordinary, horrible war. Concentration camps, slaughter, atomic bombs, people killed for nothing. That can make anybody a little pessimistic."

Abraham Polonsky, Writer/Director of *Force of Evil* (1948)

Still from 'M' (1931)
Hans Beckert (Peter Lorre, right) leads Elsie Beckmann (Inge Landgut) to her death. He is the archetypal film killer, a mixture of guilt and innocence, who says at one point, "I always feel that somebody is following me... It is I myself... Following me."

The answer lies in the richness and complexity of the movement. The term 'film noir' itself was coined by the French, always astute critics and avid fans of American culture from Alexis de Tocqueville through Charles Baudelaire to the young turks at *Cahiers du cinéma*. It began to appear in French film criticism almost immediately after the conclusion of World War Two. Under Nazi occupation the French had been deprived of American movies for almost five years; and when they finally began to watch them in late 1945, they noticed a darkening not only of mood but of subject matter. Reviewers Nino Frank and Jean-Pierre Chartier wrote about these films in 1946. In 1955, long before film noir was discussed in any English-language book or article, Raymond Borde and Etienne Chaumeton wrote the first full-length study of the subject, *Panorama du film noir américain*. The young critic-film-makers at the French film periodical *Cahiers du cinéma* – Claude Chabrol, François Truffaut, Jean-Luc Godard and Eric Rohmer, to name a few – took up the cause in the late 1950s and early 1960s. They began to examine the work of noir directors like Nicholas

Mann. Americans did not catch up with the French in their perception and appreciation of noir until a new generation of film enthusiasts entered film schools in the late 1960s. As they rebelled against the canon of American film history promoted by critics like Arthur Knight and Lewis Jacobs, these film students found inspiration in neglected noir classics such as the films featured in this book: *Double Indemnity*, *Out of the Past* (1947), *T-Men* (1948), *Detour* (1945), *Criss Cross* (1949), *Gun Crazy* (1950), *Touch of Evil* (1958), *In a Lonely Place* (1950), *The Reckless Moment* (1949) and *Kiss Me Deadly* (1955). The publication of several essays in English on noir, most importantly Raymond Durgnat's 'Paint It Black: The Family Tree of Film Noir' (*Cinema* 6/7, August 1970) and Paul Schrader's 'Notes on Film Noir' (*Film Comment* 8, Spring 1972), followed in the early 1970s. Still, when the first comprehensive survey of film noir in English, *Film Noir, An Encyclopedic Reference to the American Style*, first appeared in 1979, the term 'film noir' was still mostly unknown outside of film school circles. Finally, with the added impact of a burgeoning neo-noir movement in the 1980s, the mainstream press took up the term. By the time the Terminator blasted through a nightclub called Tech Noir in 1984, the debate over what constitutes film noir was in full swing.

All critics can agree that film noir's roots are deep and diverse. On the literary side, noir drew heavily from the works of the hard-boiled school of detective fiction written by the likes of Dashiell Hammett, Raymond Chandler, James M. Cain, David Goodis and Cornell Woolrich. Also influential were the writings of naturalist authors like Emile Zola and Ernest Hemingway, the latter being a particularly potent role model with his clipped and poetic prose style and pointed dialogue. It is no coincidence that the works of these writers were among the first adapted, beginning with Hammett's *The Maltese Falcon* in 1941, Woolrich's *Phantom Lady* (1944), Cain's *Double Indemnity* (1944) and *The Postman Always Rings Twice* (1946), Chandler's *Farewell, My Lovely* (as *Murder, My Sweet*, 1944) and *The Big Sleep* (1946), Hemingway's *The Killers* (1946) and Goodis' *Dark Passage* (1947).

On the artistic side, German expressionism, with its chiaroscuro lighting, distorted camera angles and symbolic designs, was probably the single most important influence on the look of film noir. The silent films that followed *Das Kabinett des Dr Caligari* (*The Cabinet of Dr Caligari*, 1919) from directors like Fritz Lang (*Metropolis* (1926), the Dr Mabuse series) and F.W. Murnau (*Nosferatu* (1922), *Der Letzte Mann* (*The Last Laugh*, 1924)) were greatly admired in the American film industry, as becomes obvious when one looks at the Universal horror films of the early 1930s. It is natural that the values of expressionism would seep into this already dark movement, but there is an even greater reason for its influence, because many of the most prominent directors of film noir in the classic period – Fritz Lang, Otto Preminger, Robert Siodmak, Billy Wilder, Edgar G. Ulmer, Max Ophüls, Jacques Tourneur and Jean Renoir – were émigrés from Europe. They had worked in Germany and France where expressionism and poetic realism had been the dominant artistic movements for over a decade. What could be more natural than to apply the techniques of those movements, particularly when faced with the psychologically perverse and often fatalistic stories of the hard-boiled writers, as they created the noir cycle?

On the philosophical level, the 1930s and early 1940s saw both existentialism and Freudian psychology make inroads beyond American literature and into mainstream newspapers and magazines. Existentialist novels such as Jean-Paul

ABOVE
On the set of 'Attack!' (1956)
Director Robert Aldrich holds a copy of 'Panorama du film noir', the first book about film noir.

PAGES 12/13
Still from 'Quai des brumes' (1938)
The French poetic realist films of the 1930s mixed romantic crime thrillers with fatalism in low-life, fog-shrouded settings. Here deserter Jean (Jean Gabin) tries to save Nelly (Michèle Morgan) from a life of crime.

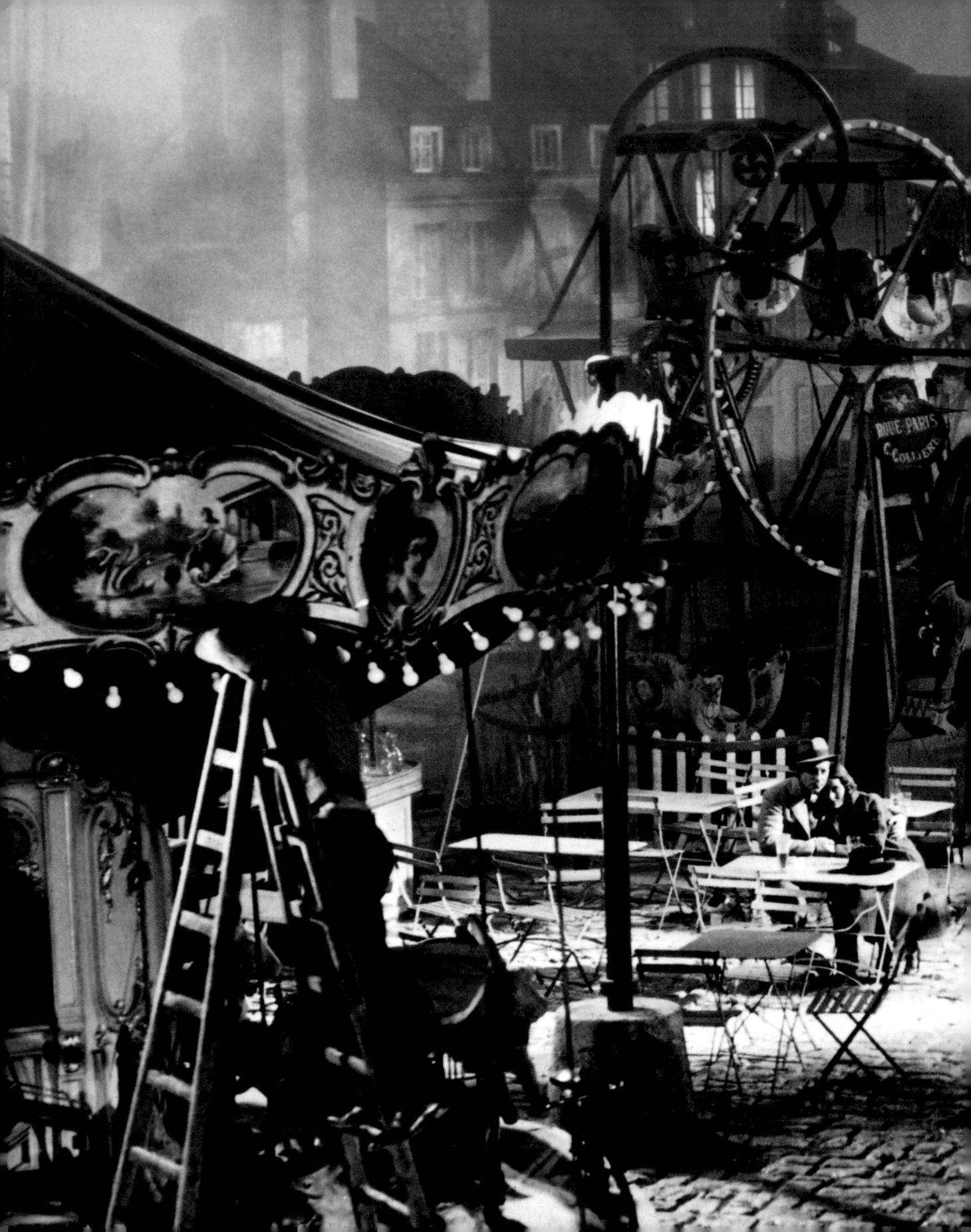

Sartre's *La Nausée* (*Nausea*, 1938) were already on the shelves in the libraries of the intelligentsia. Psychology journals dealt extensively with Freud's theories while more and more of the upper-middle class, which included the film community, were finding their way onto the couches of analysts. Both these theories helped promote a worldview that stressed the absurdity of existence along with the importance of the individual's past in determining his or her actions, views which found a receptive audience in a country wracked first by economic depression and then by world war. Two of the most important themes of the noir movement, 'the haunted past' and 'the fatalistic nightmare,' draw directly from these two sources.

In a genre there are icons which reoccur and allow the viewer to identify an individual film as part of a type. With a movement a wider and richer assortment of indicators are in play. Film noir is much more than darkly lit crime films reeking of sex and violence, as perceived by contemporary reviewers. As a cycle of films, they rely as much, if not more, on the elements of style as they do on content. In terms of narrative, they gravitate more significantly around complex themes and not mere icons.

Themes

The Haunted Past. Noir protagonists are seldom creatures of the light. They are often escaping some past burden, sometimes a traumatic incident from their past (as in *Detour* or *Touch of Evil*) or sometimes a crime committed out of passion (as in *Out of the Past*, *Criss Cross* and *Double Indemnity*). Occasionally, they are simply fleeing their own demons created by ambiguous events buried in the past, as in *In a Lonely Place*. Whatever the source of the problem, these characters seek concealment in the dark alleys and dimly lit rooms that proliferate in the world of noir. The past to a noir protagonist is no fleeting phantom. It is real and tangible and menacing. In the noir world both past and present are inextricably bound, as it is in the novels of the great French writer Marcel Proust and the work of pulp romantic Raymond Chandler (who called Proust a 'connoisseur of degenerates'). One cannot escape one's past, no matter how much he or she might try. And only in confronting it can the noir protagonist hope for some kind of redemption, even if it is at the end of a gun.

The Fatalistic Nightmare. The noir world revolves around causality. Events are linked like an unbreakable chain and lead inevitably to a heavily foreshadowed conclusion. It is a deterministic universe in which psychology (*In a Lonely Place*, *The Reckless Moment*), chance (*Detour*, *Double Indemnity*) and even the structures of society (*Touch of Evil*, *T-Men*) can ultimately override whatever good intentions and high hopes the main characters may have.

Archetypes

Film noir has its share of character types. Among them are:

The Truth Seeker. While it may belie the popular conception, the truth seeker in film noir is not primarily a private investigator in the mould of Chandler's Philip Marlowe or Hammett's Sam Spade. He is often an officer of the law (*Touch of Evil*, *T-Men*), a criminal (*Detour*, *Criss Cross*, *Double Indemnity*), rarely a woman (*The Reckless Moment* being one of the exceptions) and, outside of Hammett and Chandler, seldom a private investigator (*The Dark Corner* (1946), *Kiss Me Deadly*).

ABOVE
Still from 'Pépé le Moko' (1937)
The first poetic realist film, 'Pépé le Moko' has a delicate and menacing use of light and setting that set the standard for others to follow.

OPPOSITE
Still from 'Pépé le Moko' (1937)
Whilst in Algiers' Casbah, Pépé (Jean Gabin) can easily elude the police. However, after meeting a Parisian tourist he longs for his freedom and to catch the boat home. In the final moments, having been lured out of the Casbah, Pépé must watch his boat sail away.

ABOVE
Still from 'La nuit du carrefour' (1932)
Some nice location filming enhances this adaptation of the Georges Simenon novel.

OPPOSITE
Still from 'La chienne' (1931)
In his search for tenderness Maurice Legrand (Michel Simon) is outraged when he finds his mistress Lucienne Pelletier (Janie Marèse) in bed with another man, so he kills her and lets the other lover take the blame. This Jean Renoir film was remade by Fritz Lang in America as 'Scarlet Street' (1945).

The truth seeker can wear any costume, for his and sometimes her primary goal is to navigate the convoluted maze of the noir universe to find a critical answer, perhaps to discover a 'great what's-it,' as the object of the search in *Kiss Me Deadly* is dubbed.

The Hunted. Growing out of the influence of existentialism combined with the fatalism inherent in much of German expressionism, the noir protagonist is frequently pursued and hunted from beginning to end of a film. He is usually a male and an outsider, much like Albert Camus' Meursault in his novel *L'Etranger* (*The Outsider*, 1942). He finds it difficult to connect with a universe which seems so ruled by chance, so inherently absurd. Like Meursault, he may find himself drawn to rebellious criminal acts in defiance of this absurdity.

The Femme Fatale. The most subversive element in most film noirs is the female character, who is often a femme fatale. In recent decades feminist critics like Camille Paglia in *Vamps and Tramps* (1994) and the contributors to the landmark study *Women in Film Noir* (1978) have reclaimed the femme fatale, the black widow, the spider woman, from the male perception of evil and castrating bitch. They have seen instead many powerful and seductive characters who provide a possible female alternative to the male rebel. In the femme fatale's case, the object of her derision, rather than an absurd universe, may be male patriarchy. Post-feminist critics have analyzed characters like Phyllis Dietrichson in *Double Indemnity,* Vera in *Detour* and Anna in *Criss Cross* and found strong women trapped in a male-dominated universe, who were willing to use any weapon, including their own sexuality, to level the playing field.

Visual Iconography

The visual look of film noir can be traced from the street paintings of Edward Hopper and Reginald Marsh to the grisly crime photos of Weegee. Simply put, what most viewers notice when watching a noir movie are:

Chiaroscuro Lighting. Low-key lighting, in the style of Rembrandt or Caravaggio, marks most noirs of the classic period. Shade and light play against each other not only in night exteriors but also in dim interiors shielded from daylight by curtains or Venetian blinds. Hard, unfiltered side-light and rim light outline and reveal only a portion of a face to create a dramatic tension all its own. Cinematographers such as Nicholas Musuraca, John F. Seitz and John Alton took this style to the highest level in films like *Out of the Past, Double Indemnity* and *T-Men.* Their black and white photography with its high contrasts, stark day exteriors and realistic night work became the standard of the noir style.

Odd Angles. Noir cinematographers favoured low angles for several reasons. Firstly, this angle made the characters rise from the ground in an almost expressionistic manner, giving them dramatic girth and symbolic overtones. In addition, it also allowed the viewer to see the ceilings of the interior settings, creating even more of a sense of claustrophobia and paranoia, appropriate emotions for the world of noir. High angles could also produce disequilibrium, peering down a stairwell over a flimsy railing or out of a skyscraper window at a city street far below.

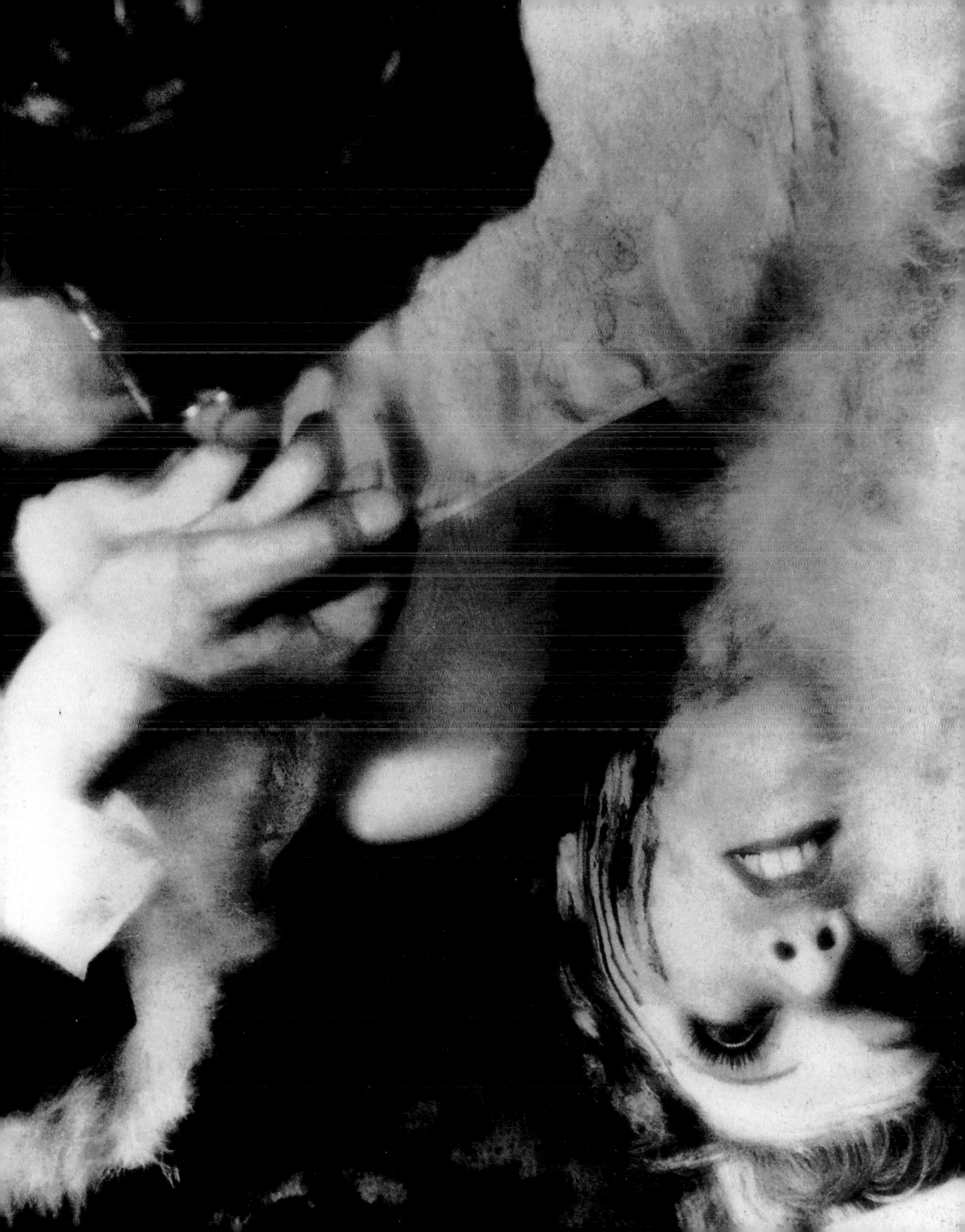

Moving Camera. For directors like Ophüls and Lang, the camera that slides across a room past an array of foreground clutter or tracks a character through a crowded café had a relentless and fateful quality. When combined with a long take, suspenseful sequences were subtly enhanced.

The Urban Landscape. Noir films are most often set in the urban landscape, particularly the cities of Los Angeles, New York and San Francisco. The metropolis with its circles of light under sidewalk lamps, dim alleyways, a press of shadowy pedestrians and wet, grimy streets is the perfect milieu for the nightmarish events of noir. From the footsteps that resonate off the concrete and track the woman alone in *Phantom Lady* to the flashing neon outside a killer's hotel room in *The Unsuspected* (1947), ordinary sights and sounds acquire a sinister context in the noir universe. And when the setting shifts to rural landscapes as in *Out of the Past, On Dangerous Ground* (1952), *Storm Fear* (1956) or *Nightfall* (1957) the idyllic contrasts to urban corruption can become either a sanctuary or a killing ground.

Flashback and Subjective Camera. Whether introduced via a ripple effect or simply a smash cut, the past palpably intrudes in film noir via flashback. The flashback can be filtered through a single character's point of view (*Criss Cross*) or ostensibly detached and objective (*The Killing*, 1956): seeing the past gives a reality that no amount of telling can match.

Diction

Noir films draw their verbal power from the hard-boiled school of writing.

Hard-bitten Poetry. Quotable noir lines abound in books on the subject. The dialogue of noir movies is rife with characters who 'crack wise,' from *double enten-dres* to poetic conceits. The first meeting between insurance agent Walter Neff and femme fatale Phyllis Dietrichson in *Double Indemnity* is a classic example. Neff's opening voice-over features this piece of hard-bitten doggerel: "There was no way I could have known that murder sometimes can smell like honeysuckle." And once inside the Dietrichson house the celebrated, sexually loaded exchange between Neff and Phyllis begins:

Neff: I wish you'd tell me what's engraved on that anklet.
Phyllis: Just my name.
Neff: As for instance?
Phyllis: Phyllis.
Neff: Phyllis, huh. I think I like that.
Phyllis: But you're not sure.
Neff: I'd have to drive it around the block a couple of times.
Phyllis (Standing up): Mr. Neff, why don't you drop by tomorrow evening around 8:30? He'll be in then.
Neff: Who?
Phyllis: My husband. You were anxious to talk to him, weren't you?
Neff: Yeah, I was. But I'm sort of getting over the idea, if you know what I mean.
Phyllis: There's a speed limit in this state, Mr. Neff, 45 miles an hour.
Neff: How fast was I going, Officer?
Phyllis: I'd say around 90.

"The plot didn't matter at all. All we were trying to do was make every scene entertain. I can't follow the story. I saw some of it on TV the other night and I'd listen to some of the things [Bogart] would talk about and it had me thoroughly confused."

Producer/Director Howard Hawks about *The Big Sleep* [1]

Still from 'The Beast of the City' (1932)
Captain James Fitzpatrick asks his no-good brother Ed to keep an eye on Daisy Stevens (Jean Harlow) so that gangster Sam Belmonte can be brought to justice.

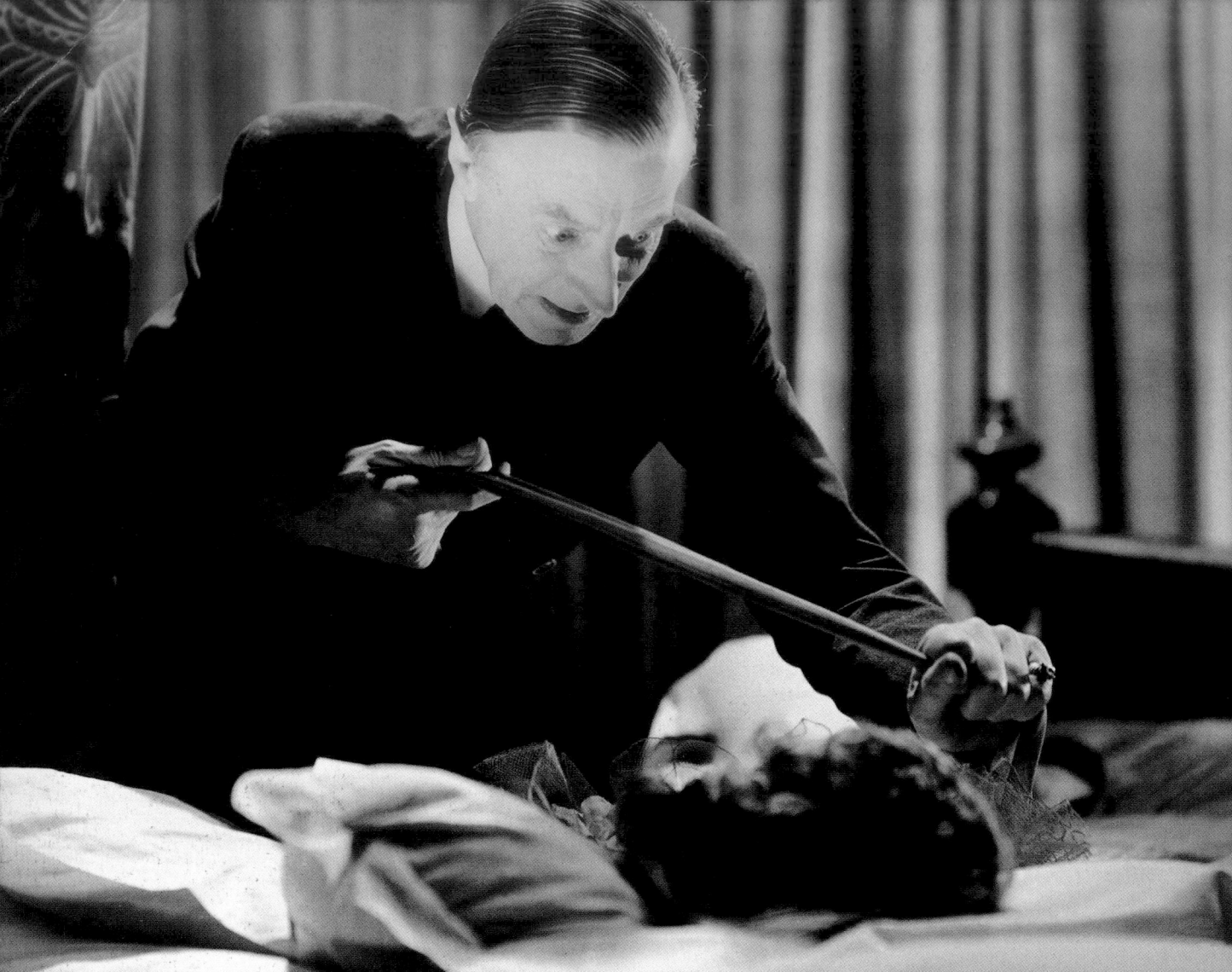

Still from 'They Drive by Night' (1938)
Killer Walter Hoover (Ernest Thesiger) at work in this rather nasty English film. As with 'M' and 'La chienne,' the story is concerned with how the main characters interact with society.

Neff: Suppose you get down off your motorcycle and give me a ticket.
Phyllis: Suppose I let you off with a warning this time.
Neff: Suppose it doesn't take.
Phyllis: Suppose I have to whack you over the knuckles.
Neff: Suppose I bust out crying and put my head on your shoulder.
Phyllis: Suppose you try putting it on my husband's shoulder.
Neff: That tears it...

Voice-over Narration. First-person narration was a popular device among the hard-boiled writers. It accomplished several purposes in noir films. First of all, it put the viewer into the mind of the protagonist. In that way the viewer could experience in a more intimate way the angst of the character. More importantly, it compelled the viewer to identify at least partly with the narrator, even when that narrator was deeply flawed, capable of criminal behaviour or even psychopathic rage as in so many of the classic noir works.

As we move further into the 21st century, this enthusiasm for film noir continues unabated. On television, a large number of series from the original *Dragnet* (1951–1959) to *NYPD Blue* (1993–) assimilate a noir ethos into their own particular genre. On radio, Garrison Keillor's *A Prairie Home Companion* features a weekly vignette devoted to a character called Guy Noir, Private Eye. In literature, neo-noir and neo-hard-boiled writers like James Ellroy (*L.A. Confidential*, 1990) dominate the mystery-suspense markets. From cinema to computer games to comic books, in the US and around the world, the pervasive influence of noir is lurking in the shadows constantly ready to emerge and colour – or rather to reduce to the monochrome of black and white – any plot, character or image. What is this thing called noir? Hopefully this book will provide a few clues to a definition, will present some details that hint at its depth and breadth and will lead the reader back to the films. For that is where one can locate the scenes that fired the imaginations of audiences of the classic period, that stunned Frenchmen Frank and Chartier with their violent tone, that inspired a new generation of film-makers with their grim philosophy, where one can find the heart of that particular darkness known as film noir.

Still from 'The Stranger on the Third Floor' (1940)
Reporter Mike Ward (John McGuire) sees The
Stranger (Peter Lorre) running away from a
murder scene. As a result Mike is put in jail for
murder and his girlfriend has to clear him. This is
often cited as the first American film noir
because of the voice-over, the shadowy
camerawork, the wrong man being accused and
the highly expressionistic nightmare sequence.

The Perfect Crime

Conspiracy and betrayal, love and sex, murder and the perfect crime – all are linchpins of film noir, all are part of the plot of *Double Indemnity*. Certainly murder for profit or murder for love are conceits much older than the noir cycle; but as a tale of murder that combines the two, *Double Indemnity* is for many the quintessential film noir. Still, just as nature may abhor a vacuum, the noir cycle certainly abhors a perfect crime. In fact, noir seldom paints a picture of perfection. The failure of would-be perfect criminals is a more likely result, or as *Double Indemnity*'s protagonist, Walter Neff, puts it when he begins his narration: "Yes, I killed him. I killed him for money and for a woman. I didn't get the money and I didn't get the woman. Pretty, isn't it?"

Pretty it's not. In fact, the sordidness of *Double Indemnity* is counter-balanced only by the serendipitous elements that came together and permitted it to be made. On the surface, the film's origins go back to a novella of the same name by James M. Cain, which first appeared serialized over eight issues of *Liberty* magazine in 1935–1936. Of course, there is also Cain's first novel, *The Postman Always Rings Twice* (1934), to be considered, because it is a remarkably similar tale of murder for money and for a woman. But long before that – before his first book, a non-fiction treatise on *Our Government* – Cain was a reporter for the *New York World* and one of many such to attend the sensational 1927 trial of Ruth Snyder and Judd Grey, a pair of real-life, would-be perfect criminals who turned on each other and went to the electric chair.

From that real event, Cain fashioned two stories which were soon optioned by Hollywood. But neither Paramount, which owned the novella, nor M.G.M., which had purchased the rights to *Postman*, could get a script past Joe Breen, the head of the Hays Office which enforced the motion picture code. Not until World War Two put things in perspective, that is. Even then *Double Indemnity* might have turned out quite differently. If Billy Wilder's regular collaborator, Charles Brackett, had not loathed the material, then Wilder would not have looked for another co-writer. If Cain had not been under contract to a rival studio then Raymond Chandler would not have been hired as Wilder's collaborator. If Chandler had lost his temper at Wilder's countless slights and plunged a letter-opener into the director's back... In the end, with Fred MacMurray being cast after George Raft and Alan Ladd had passed, with Barbara Stanwyck in a hand-me-down blonde wig from Marlene

Still from 'Double Indemnity' (1944)
Insurance agent Walter Neff (Fred MacMurray) and Phyllis Dietrichson (Barbara Stanwyck) kill her husband for his life insurance. They are together now "to the end of the line."

'I make no conscious effort to be tough, or hard-boiled, or grim, or any of the things I am usually called. I merely try to write as the character would write, and I never forget that the average man, from the fields, the streets, the bars, the offices and even the gutters of his country, has acquired a vividness of speech that goes beyond anything I could invent.'

James M. Cain, Preface to *Double Indemnity* (1943)

and Edward G. Robinson, all cast somewhat against type. Then there are the contents: ironic, first-person narration; extensive flashbacks organized around that; a femme fatale; greed that leads to murder; as forthright a portrayal of adultery as the Hays Office would permit; several other 'pairings,' not just the old/young attractions of Neff & Lola and Phyllis & Zachetti but also Neff & Keyes; a savvy investigator; finally, betrayal and death (actual and implied) for the illicit lovers. (It also garnered more Academy Award nominations than any other film noir – no wins, of course.)

As early 1945, Lloyd Shearer's *New York Times* article identified *Double Indemnity* as the beginning of 'a trend in Hollywood toward the wholesale production of lusty, hard-boiled, gut-and-gore crime stories, all fashioned on a theme with a combination of plausibly motivated murder and studded with high-powered Freudian implication.' Jean-Pierre Chartier, the French critic who first asserted that 'Americans also make noir films' in 1946, agreed with Raft that the movie had no 'good guy' and that 'all the characters are more or less venal.' Chartier singled out 'black widow' Phyllis Dietrichson as 'particularly monstrous': 'when things get complicated, she tries to kill her insurance agent accomplice; and the film hasn't yet reached its climax before we further learn that, while all this was going on, she was having an affair with her step-daughter's fiancé.' There are, in fact, few women in film noir who would rival Phyllis. Jane Palmer in *Too Late for Tears* (1949), who kills a corrupt private detective and her own husband (and probably killed her first husband as well), is a distant second. Nino Frank, the other French critic credited with the earliest definition of film noir in 1946, was struck by 'this hardness, this misogyny, in *Double Indemnity*. There is no mystery here, we know everything from the beginning, and we follow the preparation for the crime, its execution and its aftermath. Consequently our interest is focused on the characters, and the narrative unfolds with a striking clarity that is sustained throughout.'

Double Indemnity opens with an unusual title sequence. While Miklós Rózsa's stentorian minor chords portend some vague doom, the silhouette of a man on crutches moves towards the camera. In the opening shots of the picture, a car speeds through a downtown area at night and stops in front of a large office building. The driver is Walter Neff, insurance salesman and wounded criminal. Upstairs in the offices of his firm, he tells his story to a dictaphone. From the first the tone is far different from Cain. While the voice-over provides a ready equivalent to the novel's first person prose, Cain reveals the situation more obliquely, the first hint coming halfway through the opening chapter: 'All of a sudden she looked at me and I felt a chill creep up my back and into the roots of my hair. "Do you sell accident insurance?"'

For all its notoriety, Cain's novella was fairly tame. The 'vividness of speech' of his Walter Huff (the film's Walter Neff) consists of some occasional argot and misuse of some third person plural verbs with third person singular subjects. The ending in which Huff and Mrs. Nirdlinger (the film's Mrs. Dietrichson) execute a suicide pact on the high seas is more soap opera than noir. Wilder and Chandler did a lot more

Still from 'The Lady From Shanghai' (1948)
Stupid sailor Michael O'Hara (Orson Welles, right) is used as bait for sharks Arthur and Elsa Bannister (Everett Sloane and Rita Hayworth). Once the sharks smell blood they rip each other to shreds in the famous funhouse mirror shootout.

ABOVE
Still from 'Human Desire' (1954)
Carl Buckley (Broderick Crawford) beats his wife
Vicki (Gloria Grahame) because he is jealous of
her suspected sexual liaisons. This is all the
more frustrating for him because Vicki withholds
sexual favours from him.

RIGHT
On the set of 'Human Desire' (1954)
Director Fritz Lang (left) tries to find the most
effective angle for the shot.

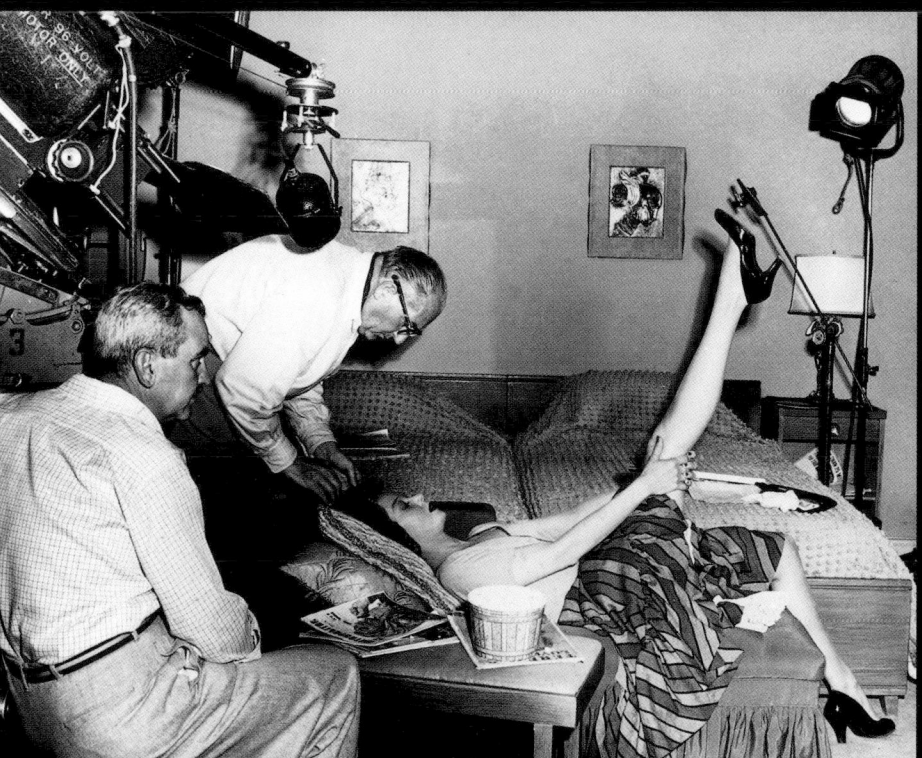

Still from 'Human Desire' (1954)
After Carl commits murder, he binds Vicki to him with blackmail. She tries to extricate herself from her husband by persuading Jeff Warren (Glenn Ford) to kill him. Fritz Lang used the intersecting railway tracks as a symbol of the way the characters intermingle.

On the set of 'Human Desire' (1954)
Although Gloria Grahame was more overtly sexual than Simone Simon in Jean Renoir's 1938 film version of Emile Zola's novel, the French film was more frank about the sexual perversions of the characters. Cinematographer Burnett Guffey, who lensed over 20 film noirs, is on the left.

Still from 'Double Indemnity' (1944)
Cinematographer John F. Seitz also shot director
Billy Wilder's 'The Lost Weekend' and 'Sunset
Boulevard', and other film noirs.

*"By the time of shooting we generally had a pretty
good idea of the mood we wanted. There was a
lot of night work in* This Gun for Hire, *and we
just kept that style throughout. You know I saw*
Double Indemnity *the other night; and it's almost
a perfect picture."*

Cinematographer John F. Seitz [2]

Still from 'Double Indemnity' (1944)
Phyllis: "We're both rotten."
Walter: "Only you're more rotten. Good-bye baby."
They shoot each other.

than change the names, and their voice-over narration is repeatedly more chilling than any moment in the book. While the basic plot is retained, the film's relationship between Neff and his mentor Keyes is more sharply focused. For Neff more than for Huff, the desire for a woman and for money are confounded with the desire to beat Keyes, to overcome a powerful father figure. Huff's manuscript is not addressed to Keyes. If he hopes for any reader it would be Lola, the daughter of his victim. Wallowing in self-deception, Huff writes: 'Maybe she'll see it sometime and not think so bad of me after she understands how it all was.' Huff's movie-self, Neff, understands the score. Does he really still think he can get away after he leaves the story on Keyes' dictaphone? Does it matter? As Neff says in voice-over after everything has gone as planned, "suddenly it came over me that everything would go wrong. It sounds crazy, Keyes, but it's true so help me: I couldn't hear my own footsteps. It was the walk of a dead man."

The fatalistic tone of *Double Indemnity*, the subtle sense of malaise which made such an impression on the French critics in 1946, is sustained as much by its naturalistic and hardbitten performances as through its visual style. Certainly the final deadly embrace of Neff and Phyllis in the parlour would not be the same were it not lit only by the thin shafts of light that manage to pierce the closed Venetian blinds. But the screen presence of the actors is what sells the moment. The perfect

"Suddenly it came over me that everything would go wrong. It sounds crazy, Keyes, but it's true, so help me. I couldn't hear my own footsteps. It was the walk of a dead man."

Walter Neff (Fred MacMurray) to Barton Keyes (Edward G. Robinson) in *Double Indemnity* (1944)

"I shot that whole thing in the gas chamber, the execution, when everything was still, with tremendous accuracy. But then I realized, look this thing is already over. I just already have one tag outside that office, when Neff collapses on the way to the elevator, where he can't even light the match. And from the distance, you hear the sirens, be it an ambulance or be it the police, you know it is over. No need for the gas chamber."

Billy Wilder [3]

crime having eluded them, Neff and Phyllis suffer the fate predicted by his mentor Keyes:

"Murder is never perfect. It always comes apart sooner or later. When two people are involved, it's usually sooner... And it's not like taking a trolley ride together where they can get off at different stops. They're stuck with each other and they've got to ride all the way to the end of the line and it's a one-way trip and the last stop is the cemetery."

Billy Wilder

On the set of 'Double Indemnity' (1944)
Billy Wilder instructs Barbara Stanwyck on how
to make femme fatale Phyllis Dietrichson as
sleazy as possible.

Billy Wilder was born Samuel Wilder on 22 June 1906 in Sucha, which was then in
the Austro-Hungarian Empire but is now Poland. He was nicknamed 'Billie' after
Buffalo Bill Cody. After a year studying law, he began a career as a journalist at a
Viennese newspaper, then moved to Germany in 1927 and found work as a reporter
for a variety of Berlin's tabloids and magazines. He wrote several screenplays before
working as a screenwriter on *Menschen am Sonntag* (*People on Sunday*, 1929).
Despite this success, his Jewish heritage forced him to flee Germany in 1933. During
a year in France he was co-director of *Mauvaise Graine* (*Bad Seed*, 1934) but soon
moved on to the United States. Settling in Hollywood and rooming with actor Peter
Lorre, Wilder learned English. In 1934 he was one of the adapters of the musical
Music in the Air directed by fellow émigré Joe May. He began a writing partnership
with Charles Brackett on *That Certain Age* (1938), then came under the tutelage of
Ernst Lubitsch, first with *Bluebeard's Eighth Wife* (1938) and then with *Ninotchka*
(1939), for which he received his first Academy Award nomination. Wilder's success
as a writer forced Paramount to give him a chance to direct the 1942 comedy *The
Major and the Minor*. *Double Indemnity* was his third feature. His fourth, *The Lost
Weekend* (1945), earned him two Oscars as writer and director. *Sunset Boulevard*

MORE FOR LESS

(1950) was the final collaboration with Brackett and most of his features thereafter were dark comedies, usually written with I.A.L. Diamond. Wilder enjoyed critical and commercial success – a career total of 21 Academy Awards nominations and six wins – until his 'retirement' in 1981. In 1986 he received the American Film Institute's Life Achievement Award and in 1988 the Irving G. Thalberg Award. He died at his home in Beverly Hills, California on 27 March 2002.

On the set of 'Double Indemnity' (1944)
Wartime food shortages meant that security guards were posted to protect the real cans of food in the grocery store. Despite this, a can of peaches and four bars of soap went missing.

"I don't make only one kind of movie, and I am not aware of patterns. We're not aware that 'This picture will be in this genre.' You're trying to make as good and as entertaining a picture as you possibly can. If you have any kind of style, the discerning ones will detect it."

Billy Wilder [4]

The Fatalistic Nightmare

The world of noir is at its core a nightmare world. It is filled with odd synchronicities, unexplained events and chance encounters, creating a chain of events that ultimately drags its unlucky protagonists to their foreshadowed end. Some may at the last moment escape their nightmare and return to relative normality. Such is the case with the unjustly accused businessman in Robert Siodmak's *Phantom Lady* (1944), who is rescued from his fate through the ingenious efforts of his secretary (Ella Raines), or the straying husband (Dick Powell) in Andre de Toth's *Pitfall* (1948), whose salvation from the noir underworld comes about through a series of chance events. But most, like Neff in *Double Indemnity* or Edward G. Robinson's Christopher Cross (his name alone speaks volumes) in Fritz Lang's brilliant *Scarlet Street* (1945), or Frank Bigelow (Edmond O'Brien) in *DOA* (1950), are doomed to follow the maze-like convolutions of their stories to the bitter end. Neff seals his own fate when he so easily falls for the femme fatale of the piece, Phyllis Dietrichson. All his actions from then on seem designed to lead him to his foreshadowed end, bleeding to death on the floor of the insurance company he tried to cheat. Cross also lets lust determine his actions as he becomes the virtual slave of his own femme fatale, Kitty (Joan Bennett). The audience see the inexorable devolution of this sympathetic if foolish dreamer, as he paints her toenails or sets her up in a lavish apartment. Bigelow's fate is probably the most arbitrary and absurd in the classic existentialist definition of that word. He wakes up one morning to find he has been poisoned and has only a few days to live. He spends the remainder of the film finding the men responsible and learns with bitter irony before he dies that his poisoning was actually intended for another victim.

Detour, directed by Z-budget noir specialist Edgar G. Ulmer, has that same sense of the absurd. Told in flashback with a flat, depressed voice-over so typical of noir, the film traces the chain of events that led Al Roberts to the state we see him in now: dishevelled, unshaven, sullen and broke. He sits in a diner, morosely staring into a cup of coffee. A trucker puts a song on the jukebox – 'Can't Believe You Were in Love with Me' – which suddenly triggers both a violent reaction in Roberts as well as the commencement of the flashback. An expressionistic shift in the lighting of the diner sets the mood for the nightmare narrative Roberts unfolds.

The film cuts to a club in New York where Roberts plays the piano. He seems much more prosperous and even a little happier as he accompanies his girlfriend,

"Our hour is marked, and no one can claim a moment of life beyond what fate has predestined."
Napoleon

Still from 'Pitfall' (1948)
Insurance agent John Forbes (Dick Powell, left) is bored with married life, so he dallies with Mona Stevens (Lizabeth Scott) and both are menaced by lovelorn private eye MacDonald (Raymond Burr). This film is about Forbes' realisation that the American Dream is a phantom.

Sue, an attractive chanteuse who sings the tune from the jukebox. But looks are deceiving. For as Roberts walks through the preternaturally thick fog with Sue, that same sense of pessimism and doom, so evident in the first scene, pervades his persona here. Sue tells him that she wants to go to Hollywood to start a career there. He tells her bluntly that it is stupid and that she will get nowhere. As they argue the fog thickens as if to externalize Robert's own confusion about their relationship and their future plans. Ultimately he agrees to let her go, although his anger is clearly expressed in a piano piece he plays later in which he punishes the keys instead of Sue.

Roberts cannot stand to live without his lover and decides to join her but, unable to afford a ticket to Los Angeles, he must hitch-hike across the country. On the trip he is picked up by a slick, gregarious grifter named Haskell. Whilst driving Roberts notices some deep scratches on Haskell's hand. Haskell volunteers that they were given to him by "the most dangerous animal in the world – a woman," who had refused his advances and whom he literally threw out of the car. Haskell's hostility towards women makes him a clear reflection of Roberts' own latent anger towards Sue and her ability to forge her own fate while he submissively accepts his own. The two men become friendly as Haskell buys dinner and allows Roberts to drive through an intense rainstorm. When Roberts stops the car to put up the top of the

Still from 'D.O.A.' (1950)
In the exciting climax, Frank Bigelow (Edmond O'Brien, right) kills the man who killed him. The film is a race against time as Bigelow is both victim of irridium poisoning and investigator of his own murder.

convertible, Haskell falls out – dead. There is never really a feasible explanation for Haskell's death. While perhaps motivated as much by budget as by artistic choices, Ulmer has spent so much time establishing through his lighting and minimalist sets a powerfully expressionistic mood that this event just becomes another absurd chance moment in Roberts' fatalistic nightmare. Roberts panics, buries the body and takes on Haskell's identity and money so that he might continue his journey to Los Angeles and Sue.

But fate is not through with him yet or as Roberts puts it, "Whichever way you turn, fate sticks out a foot to trip you." However, it is important to note here that like the ancient Greek tragic protagonists Roberts' fate is as much created by himself as by the 'gods.' Although he seems totally unaware of it, his own tragic flaws – his anger, his pessimism, his stupidity – dovetail perfectly with fate's plan for him. Back on the desert road he spots a sultry female hitch-hiker (Vera) who is the same "dangerous animal" who had given Haskell his scars. She knows that Roberts is not Haskell and threatens to turn him in unless he goes along with her plans.

The relationship that develops between these two hitch-hikers is a perverse one. Roberts becomes literally and figuratively Vera's slave. She is abusive to him ("You don't have any brains.") while he follows behind her carrying all their baggage ("Just remember who's boss here.") She even locks the doors in their hotel room at night

"Whichever way you turn, fate sticks out a foot to trip you."

Al Roberts (Tom Neal) in *Detour* (1945)

"Say, who do you think you're talking to? A hick? Listen Mister, I've been around and I know a wrong guy when I see one. What'd you do, kiss him with a wrench?"

Vera (Ann Savage) in *Detour* (1945)

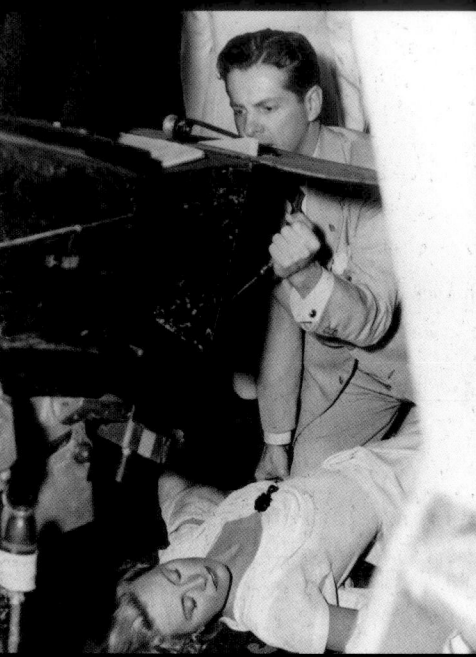

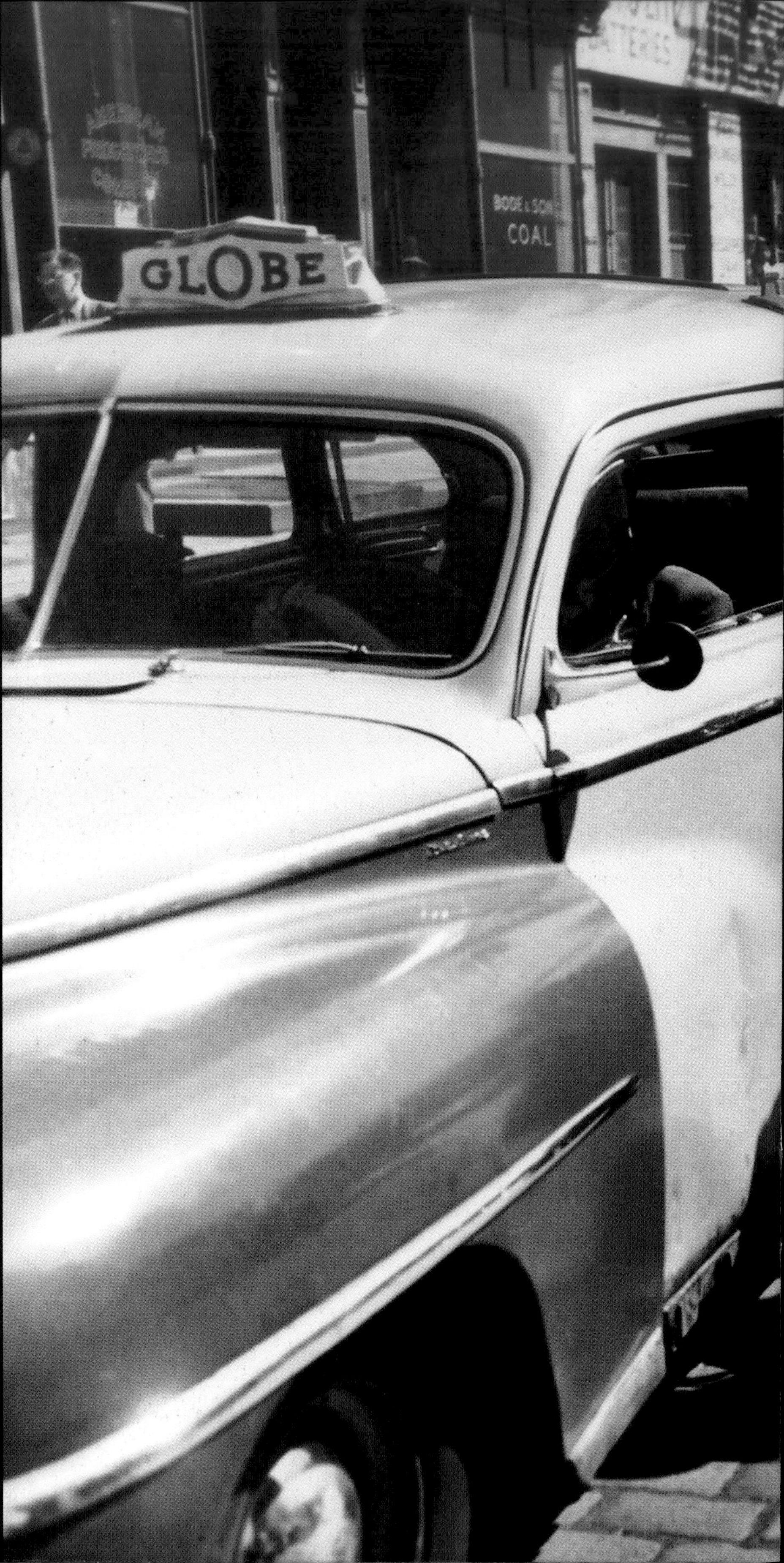

ABOVE

On the set of 'The Chase' (1946)

In an extended dream sequence Chuck Scott (Robert Cummings) is accused of killing Lorna Roman (Michèle Morgan). Chuck and Lorna eventually escape her criminal husband, but they end up at the night club where the dream murder took place.

RIGHT

Still from 'Side Street' (1950)

Courier Joe Norson (Farley Granger) is unceremoniously evicted from a taxi by George Garsell (James Craig). Norson stole an envelope full of money so that he and his pregnant wife can live the American Dream, but his conscience gets the better of him and he travels through the underbelly of American society to achieve absolution.

so he will not escape. Considering all this, Roberts accepts his fate relatively meekly. Of course, he fears that she will turn him over to the police but it is more than that. There is a level at which he believes this is just another punishment he must accept at the hands of that unjust fate he so often laments. At the same time Vera, who the viewer finds out is dying, is allowed to wreak vengeance on this man for the abuse she has suffered at the hands of men like Haskell.

On their way to Los Angeles, Vera eventually comes up with a plan to sell the car and split the money but changes her mind at the car dealership when she finds out through a newspaper that Haskell's rich father is dying. She informs Roberts that he will pose as the son and collect a fortune after the father's death. As always, Roberts is hesitant. She berates him for whining all the time, telling him that he at least has life when others (referring to herself) would gladly trade that life for the death they are heading towards. She becomes drunk and even more abusive: "Each word coming from her lips was like the crack of a whip." She grabs the phone from him and locks herself in the hotel bedroom. She falls onto the bed with the cord wrapped around her. In order to stop her from calling the police and turning him in, Roberts tries to snap the cord. In pulling it he strangles her to death. Roberts says it all: "I was cooked, done for." No one would believe that this was an accident, just as they would not have believed his story about Haskell's death, or at least that is what he thinks. It was too absurd. And so once again Roberts accepts his fate, refusing to fight back.

At the end of the film Roberts has left the diner and is back out on the road. His last fatalistic lines are recited as an appropriately black highway patrol car picks him up, "Fate or some mysterious force can put the finger on you or me for no good reason at all." Roberts' self fulfilling prophecy has at last come true.

OPPOSITE
Still from 'Fourteen Hours' (1951)
A troubled young man (Richard Basehart, in white) prepares to jump from the fifteenth floor of a New York hotel on St. Patrick's Day.

BELOW LEFT
Still from 'Nightmare Alley' (1947)
Stanton Carlisle (Tyrone Power) rises from carnival barker to crooked spiritualist by using up and spitting out everybody in his way. He meets his match in Dr. Lilith Ritter (Helen Walker), who suggests he use her confidential information during his séances, and his fall is much quicker than his rise.

BELOW
Publicity still for 'Night and the City' (1950)
Harry Fabian (Richard Widmark) only uses girlfriend Mary Bristol (Gene Tierney) as a source of money.

ABOVE
Still from 'Detour' (1945)
Told in flashback, we learn that Al Roberts (Tom Neal, at piano) wanted to follow his girlfriend singer Sue (Claudia Drake) so he hitch-hiked from New York to Los Angeles.

RIGHT
Still from 'Detour' (1945)
On the way, Al is given a lift by Charles Haskell, Jr. (Edmund MacDonald), who falls asleep and dies whilst Al is driving. Fearing that the police will not believe he is innocent, Al hides the body and drives on.

OPPOSITE
Still from 'Detour' (1945)
The shrewish Vera (Ann Savage) threatens to expose Al and then use him to claim the Haskell fortune. In desperation, Al pulls at the telephone cord whilst a drunk Vera is in the next room and he accidently strangles her. What has fate got in store for him next?

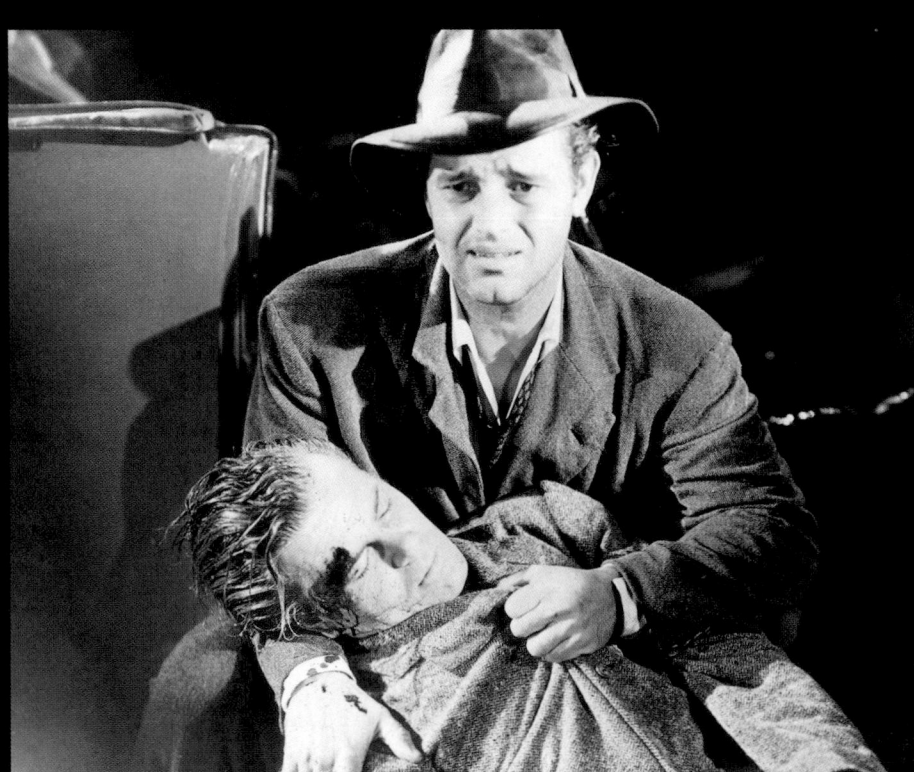

ABOVE
On the set of 'The Strange Woman' (1946)
Hedy Lamarr (centre) relaxes as Edgar G. Ulmer
(left) discusses lines with the script girl. Set in
eighteenth-century Maine, the film follows
Lamarr's wilful scheming to marry and destroy
men in order to have as much money as
possible.

RIGHT
On the set of 'Ruthless' (1948)
Edgar G. Ulmer (right) directed what some have
called a poverty-row 'Citizen Kane', about the rise
and rise of a tycoon (Zachary Scott) who has an
adding machine where his heart should be.
Assembled here with Ulmer are Louis Hayward,
Zachary Scott, Sydney Greenstreet, Lucille
Bremer, Diana Lynn and Martha Vickers.

Edgar G. Ulmer

Edgar G. Ulmer was born on 17 September 1904 in Olmütz, which was then in the Austro-Hungarian Empire and is now in the Czech republic. He studied architecture at Vienna's Academy of Arts and Sciences and philosophy at the University of Vienna. At an early age he started in theatre as an actor and set designer, including a stint with famed theatre impresario Max Reinhardt. He went to the United States in 1923 to work on Broadway. Soon he moved to Hollywood as a set designer for Universal Studios. He returned to Germany in 1925 and became an assistant to German expressionist director F.W. Murnau. Also during that time, he collaborated with future noir directors Robert Siodmak and Billy Wilder on *Menschen am Sonntag* (*People on Sunday*, 1929). After serving as production manager and editor on the Murnau/Robert Flaherty *Tabu*, Ulmer landed in Hollywood and back at Universal again, first as an art director then as director of one of the most stylish horror films of the period, *The Black Cat* (1934) starring Boris Karloff and Bela Lugosi. He soon, however, found himself on the wrong side of mogul Carl Laemmle and was gray-listed from Hollywood. He turned to low budget film-making, sometimes working as a producer or production designer, and spent the rest of his prolific career making films in almost every genre, including race films like *Moon Over Harlem* (1939) and Yiddish films like *The Light Ahead* (1939). His noir films of the 1940s, which include *Bluebeard* (1944), *Strange Illusion* (1945), *The Strange Woman* (1946) and *Ruthless* (1948), are notable for their German expressionist lighting and set design, as are his science-fiction movies such as *The Man from Planet X* (1951) and *The Amazing Transparent Man* (1960). His last noir film was *Murder is My Beat* (1955). He returned to Europe in the 1960s to make everything from low budget fantasies like *L'Atlantide* (1961) to nudist films. He died in Woodland Hills, California on 30 September 1972.

"The idea to get involved in the long road of fate – where he's an absolute loser – fascinated me. And the boy who played the leading character, Tom Neal, would end up in jail after he killed his own wife. He did practically the same thing as he did in the picture."

Edgar G. Ulmer [5]

Edgar G. Ulmer and Bela Lugosi
Ulmer (on the left) directed Boris Karloff and Bela Lugosi (on the right) in 'The Black Cat' (1934). This remarkable picture was designed in the style of 'The Cabinet of Dr. Caligari' (1919) and was scripted by Peter Ruric, who wrote noir fiction as Paul Cain.

The Burden of the Past

Noir protagonists are often individuals who are dogged by their past. In fact the burden of the past is probably one of the major themes of film noir. In Robert Siodmak's classic *The Killers* (1946), based on the short story by Ernest Hemingway, the main character Swede (Burt Lancaster) waits resignedly for his end at the hands of two thugs, knowing that his past has finally caught up with him. In *Cornered* (1945), directed and written respectively by two future blacklistees, Edward Dmytryk and Adrian Scott, Gerard (Dick Powell), after being emotionally paralyzed by the death of his wife during the war, sullenly makes his way around the world in search of the criminal or criminals he believes responsible for her demise. In *The Dark Corner* (1946), Galt, a private detective framed and imprisoned for a crime he did not commit, wallows in alienation and self-pity, rejecting human affection in order to pursue the men who betrayed him. In the back story, Galt is framed by his ex-partner and sent to prison. The film opens with his release but within days, he finds himself set up to take the fall again, this time for murder; and this time Galt doesn't even know who has framed him. The result is a prolonged cry of existential anguish distilled into Galt's classic lament to his secretary, "I feel all dead inside. I'm backed up in a dark corner and I don't know who's hitting me."

In *The Fallen Sparrow* (1943) John Garfield delivers a poignant performance as a Spanish Civil War veteran who cannot escape the memory of his period of incarceration and torture at the hands of Franco's agents. In *Tomorrow is Forever* (1945) Orson Welles plays a badly mutilated soldier who abandons his wife out of shame. Years later he finds himself drawn back to his former home. Unable either completely to escape or truly confront his past, he takes the masochistic option of assuming another identity while working at close quarters with his former wife and his own biological son. In *Cry Vengeance* (1954) Mark Stevens reprises his role from *The Dark Corner*. He is a bitter, physically and emotionally scarred cop who has decided to take vengeance on a man he believes responsible for the death of his wife and child. He is only able to shake his past through the intervention of the man he seeks. The most Freudian of all these quasi-Freudian movies is Alfred Hitchcock's *Spellbound* (1945). Psychiatrist Ingrid Bergman becomes obsessed with a patient (Gregory Peck) who has blocked out his past and the guilt associated with it. Hitchcock brings the Freudian elements to the foreground in his piece, most memorably through Salvador Dalí dream sequences that the psychiatrist must

Publicity still for 'Out of the Past' (1947)
Kathie Moffat (Jane Greer) corrupts and destroys the man who loves her, Jeff Bailey/Markham (Robert Mitchum).

'Things always seem fairer when we look back at them, and it is out of that inaccessible tower of the past that Longing leans and beckons.'

James Russell Lowell

53

ABOVE
Still from 'Out of the Past' (1947)
When private eye Jeff Markham is hired to find Kathie by Whit Sterling, the man she shot and stole from, Jeff falls for the dame. They are tracked down by Jeff's partner Jack Fisher (Steve Brodie, right).

RIGHT
Still from 'Out of the Past' (1947)
The first half of the film is told by Jeff Bailey to Ann (Virginia Huston) as he travels to Lake Tahoe to meet Whit Sterling again after three years. He tells Ann: "I'm tired of running."

"I never saw her in the daylight – we seemed to live by night. What was left of the day went away like the smoke from a pack of cigarettes."

Jeff Bailey (Robert Mitchum) in *Out of the Past* (1947)

decode in order to save her patient/lover. Even this partial list of classic period film noirs that feature characters damaged, both emotionally and physically, by past events they cannot or, more often, choose not to purge, demonstrates the prominence of the theme.

Out of the Past (1947), directed by noir veteran Jacques Tourneur, scripted by noir novelist-screenwriter Daniel Mainwaring and photographed by noir mainstay Nicholas Musuraca, says it all with its title. The protagonist, Jeff Bailey/Markham – played by noir icon Robert Mitchum – has buried himself in Bridgeport, a small town in the California mountains. There he has made a new life. He owns a garage and employs a profoundly deaf boy who looks up to him like a father. He is dating a virginal small town girl, Ann, who thinks he is "secretive" but still loves him. The setting could not be more idyllic: a glistening lake, clean mountain air, bright sunshine, sparse population, the antithesis of the cities Bailey is trying to escape. But it is a past which will not die and eventually takes on human form with the arrival of Joe, a black-overcoated hood who has been sent by Bailey's former employer, Whit Sterling, to retrieve him.

Bailey consents to return to the darkness and chaos of the city but not before he finally confesses his past to Ann in a ride to Sterling's house on Lake Tahoe, "I'm tired of running... I want to clean this up." In a flashback typical of noir, Bailey narrates laconically, almost fatalistically, the story that has led him to this impasse in his life. With the beginning of the flashback the mood and look of the film also changes entirely. The airy, day-lit mountain scenery is replaced by night exteriors and interiors, often in crowded bars, noisy nightclubs and maze-like city streets. The shift signals a descent into the dark past which so haunts this noir protagonist.

At this point the film-makers also introduce the femme fatale of the piece: Kathie Moffat. Years before, Sterling had sent Bailey, a private detective operating out of Los Angeles and San Francisco, to find Kathie, who had shot him and stolen $40,000. Bailey tracks her to Acapulco. His first vision of her visually encapsulates not only the reason for his obsession, but also why actress Jane Greer's Kathie became such a model for later femme fatales. "Then I saw her coming out of the sun," is the line of voice-over narration as Kathie enters the dark sleazy café, backlit by the sun. She moves languidly and assuredly, and sits down at a table, refusing to acknowledge Bailey's presence even though she is aware of his stare. She is cool and collected, lighting her cigarette, as Bailey approaches her with lame tourist banter peppered with tired pick-up lines. She deftly fends off his advances, only promising that she might return to a nearby café one night soon. So Bailey begins his vigil, patiently waiting like a "chump" until she returns again, this time "walk[ing] out of the moonlight." After that Bailey is hooked. "You are going to find it very easy to take me anywhere," he tells her most prophetically. And take him she does. As his affair with her develops, he lies to his employer about her whereabouts, risking his own life at the hands of Sterling's hoods. They do eventually escape Sterling and meet in a cabin in the shadowy woods on the outskirts of Los Angeles, but their plan for a future together is threatened by Fisher, Bailey's partner, who wants a piece of the money he believes Kathie has stolen. Fisher and Bailey struggle in the cabin, their bodies moving in and out of the shadows. Kathie watches on in close-up and for a brief few seconds the camera reveals a sadistic smile spreading across her face, as if she has finally lifted the mask presented to the affectionate lover and now exposed a cold-blooded killer beneath, someone who was capable of shooting her

"It's a question of drama really. Tragedy is, by definition, rather hopeless. Isn't Oedipus when you look at it, also existential? Women are fatal; but you wrote them because you could sell them. It all stemmed from that. As for Out of the Past, *the book and the film are entirely different. The film is a lot better, a lot less confused."*

Screenwriter/Novelist Daniel Mainwaring aka Geoffrey Homes [6]

ABOVE
Still from 'Out of the Past' (1947)
Jeff finds Kathie in Acapulco and waits for her in Pablo's. "I knew what a sucker I was."

PAGE 56
Still from 'I Married a Communist' (1950)
Successful Brad Collins (Robert Ryan, right) once belonged to the Communists and now they want him back. Here he tries to protect his new wife Nan (Laraine Day) and himself from Bailey (William Talman).

PAGE 57
Still from 'Tomorrow is Another Day' (1951)
Ex-con Bill Clark/Mike Lewis (Steve Cochran) tries to forget his past, but he kills his girlfriend Catherine Higgins' (Ruth Roman) new boyfriend and has to go on the run.

ex-lover Sterling as well as finishing off Fisher when Bailey cannot. She dispatches Fisher with a bullet and takes off in the car into the night.

The flashback ends as Bailey enters the Tahoe cabin and finds Kathie ensconced again with Sterling. She persuades Bailey to take a final job for Sterling, to steal some papers from a lawyer who is threatening to expose Sterling to the IRS. Even though Bailey seems to doubt her protestation that she is afraid of Sterling, his susceptible nature and lingering erotic obsession lead him to agree. It is clear that even though he tells her in a line so typical of noir's hardbitten and terse poetry, "You are like a leaf the wind blows from one gutter to another," he still finds her magnetic.

Once in San Francisco, Bailey begins to have second thoughts. He senses that he is being set up as the lawyer's murderer by Kathie and Sterling; and, of course, he is. Although he discovers their plot, Kathie again talks her way out by appealing to his doomed romanticism and sexual nature. She proposes they run away to Mexico, and he agrees. Like most noir protagonists Bailey is deeply flawed. Unlike Kathie, who is fairly strong in her resolve, *he* is the leaf blown about by the wind. Each move seems to force him deeper and deeper into a dark maze so forcefully visualized by the dark city streets of San Francisco. It is only later when Kathie tries to pin Fisher's murder on Bailey that he finally breaks the bond to her and his past,

demanding money for the records Sterling wants and which Bailey had taken from the lawyer's office.

But in the world of noir, clean exits are rarely permitted. Bailey returns to Bridgeport to hide out, only to be tracked by Joe. He is saved by the profoundly deaf boy, but no one can alter the ultimate trajectory of Bailey's fate. Only Bailey can even try to do that. He returns to Sterling to find him dead, shot by Kathie. Kathie now has the upper hand and all the money. In classic spider woman mode, much like Phyllis Dietrichson in *Double Indemnity*, she seizes control of the situation: "I never told you anything I wasn't. You just imagined it." She still desires him and blackmails him by threatening to accuse him of Fisher's murder to coerce him to return with her to Acapulco and rekindle their love affair. He seems to accept her ultimatum passively ("Build my gallows high, baby") but as they approach a police roadblock he causes her car to swerve. He is shot by Kathie as the police riddle the car with sub-machine gun bullets.

The film-makers add an upbeat note to this dark tale by freeing Ann from her own ties to the past. She asks the deaf boy whether Jeff was really running away with Kathie. He lies, nodding in the affirmative, thereby allowing Ann to move on with her own life, unburdened by the sort of memories which so haunted Jeff Bailey.

Still from 'The Dark Corner' (1946)
When P.I. Bradford Galt (Mark Stevens, right) is released from prison after serving time for a frame made by his partner Tony Jardine (Kurt Kreuger, left), he is then framed for his former partner's murder. He tells his secretary: "I feel all dead inside. I'm backed up in a dark corner and I don't know who's hitting me."

ABOVE
Still from 'The Killers' (1946)
Using multiple flashbacks, we follow an insurance investigator as he finds out how Swede (Burt Lancaster, right) went from boxer to criminal to filling station attendant, and why he accepted his death by two assassins without putting up a fight.

RIGHT
On the set of 'The Killers' (1946)
Director Robert Siodmak (right) fools around with cinematographer Woody Bredell.

OPPOSITE
Still from 'The Killers' (1946)
Swede goes to prison so that his girlfriend Kitty doesn't have to. When she doesn't write anymore, Charleston (Vince Barnett, right), tries to warn him that the relationship is over. In the end, having been emotionally destroyed by Kitty, Swede has no will to live and this is why he accepts his death so easily.

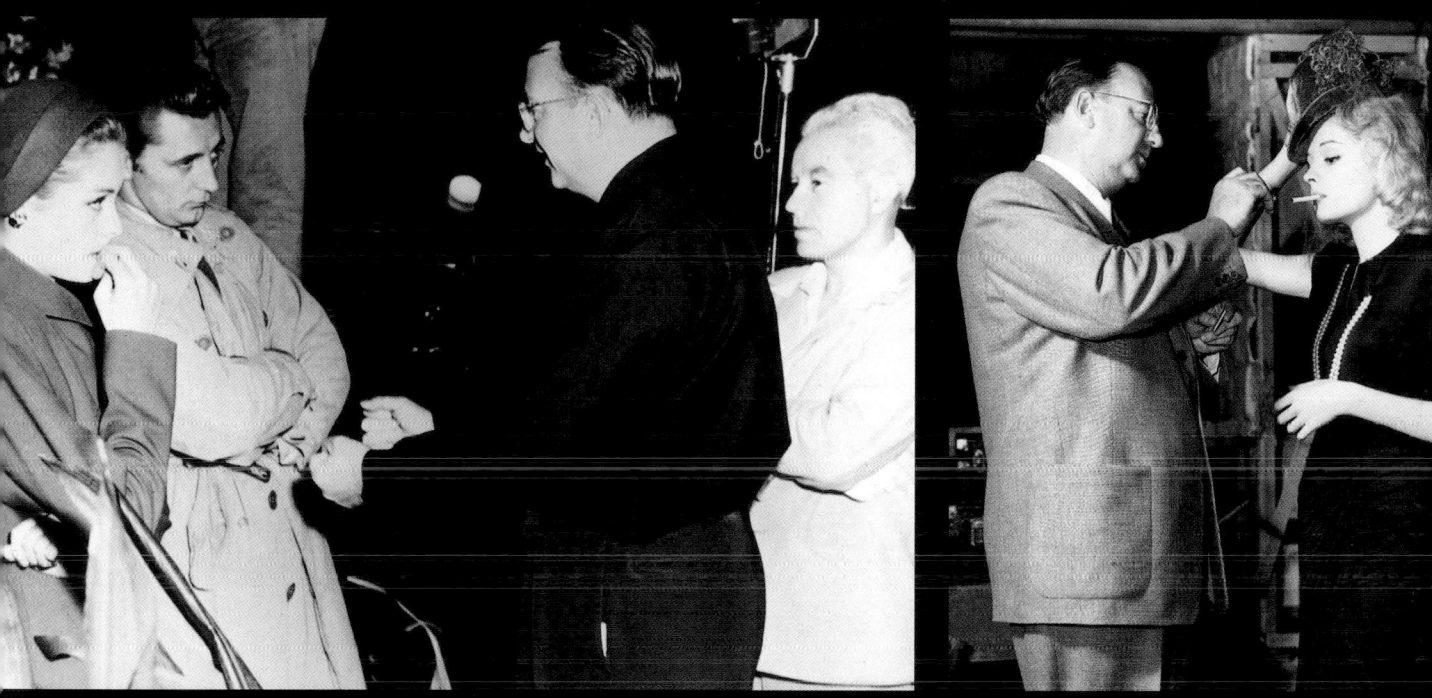

Jacques Tourneur

Jacques Tourneur was born in Paris on 12 November 1904, the son of celebrated French silent director Maurice Tourneur. He arrived in Hollywood in 1914 with his father, who began work within the Hollywood studio system. In 1924 he obtained his first movie position as an office boy at MGM. He also worked as editor and script supervisor for his father in Hollywood and later in Paris. He began his directing career in the French film industry in 1931, then returned to Hollywood in 1935 on his own and worked as a second unit director on the Pete Smith shorts at MGM, graduating to features in 1939. He left MGM to join the Val Lewton unit at RKO where he directed horror classics like *I Walked with a Zombie* (1943) and *Cat People* (1942), which established his reputation as an artful director of low budget movies. But he was never typed as simply a horror director. Tourneur worked in numerous genres. Besides *Out of the Past*, Tourneur directed *Berlin Express* (1948) and *Nightfall* (1957) based on the novel by David Goodis. He also made Westerns such as *Canyon Passage* (1946) and historical romances such as *Anne of the Indies* (1951) and *Way of a Gaucho* (1952). He returned briefly to Europe to make two features in the United Kingdom, including one of the classics of the horror genre, *Night of the Demon* (1957). Tourneur spent most of the last ten years of his career directing television with an occasional low budget feature such as the Roger Corman horror parody *The Comedy of Terrors* (1964). Tourneur retired in the late 1960s and died in France on 19 December 1977.

TOP LEFT
On the set of 'Out of the Past' (1947)
Jane Greer and Robert Mitchum listen to Jacques Tourneur give instructions about the final scene, when Jeff says: "We deserve each other." Cinematographer Nicholas Musuraca, who also lensed 'Stranger on the Third Floor', 'The Locket' and 'Deadline at Dawn', is on the right.

ABOVE
On the set of 'Out of the Past' (1947)
Jacques Tourneur helps Jane Greer try on some alternative wardrobe. Greer wanted to do more light comedy, but her characterisation in 'Out of the Past' is so compelling that it remains her bestl-known role.

OPPOSITE
Still from 'Out of the Past' (1947)
Whilst Jeff and Fisher fight, Kathie gives a slight smile and then shoots Fisher dead. She complains to Jeff that they needed Fisher dead but that Jeff would not have killed him.

"No 'big eyes.' No expressive[ness]. In the beginning you act like a nice girl. But then, after you kill the man you meet in the little house, you become a bad girl. Yes? First half, good girl. Second half, bad girl."

Director Jacques Tourneur to Jane Greer regarding her performance in *Out of the Past* **(1947)** [7]

The Caper Film

Criss Cross (1949) combines many of the themes of film noir: the obsessive or 'mad' love that dooms many fugitive couples; the first-person narration interwoven into a flashback structure; a complex heist at the core of the plot; and the simple double-cross. *The Killers*, another film by director Robert Siodmak, has a similar juxtaposition of narrative elements in which an investigator becomes fixated on finding out why a man would meet death so willingly and pieces together the story in flashback from various interviews. As in *Criss Cross*, the fate of the protagonist (portrayed in both films by Burt Lancaster) turns on a femme fatale and a betrayal after a robbery.

Several noir films released shortly after *Criss Cross* share some of these elements. While primarily a fugitive couple movie, *Gun Crazy* (1950) involves several planned capers. *White Heat* (1949) opens and closes with elaborate robberies and adds the elements of sexual duplicity and a 'brain man,' a criminal strategist who devises a plan for others to carry out. *Armored Car Robbery* and *The Asphalt Jungle* (both 1950) expand on the concept of a brain man and make him one of the principal characters. In the manner of *The Killers*, *Drive a Crooked Road* (1950) and the earlier *Framed* (1947) both use the femme fatale to lure a chump with a special skill into the criminal outfit.

While *White Heat* is certainly memorable for James Cagney's portrayal of the mother-loving, migraine suffering Cody Jarrett, its focus is on treachery rather than the planning of the heist. Jarrett's crazed exit in which he blows up a gasoline storage tank while screaming "Made it Ma. Top of the world!" reduces the structure of a caper to pure sociopathy. *The Asphalt Jungle* takes a more intellectual approach. The underlying novel by W.R. Burnett stresses the distinctions between the proletarians who actually carry out the robbery, the philosophical European who is the mastermind and the crooked lawyer who finances the enterprise to maintain an aristocratic lifestyle. John Huston's film retains much of that structure but ironically it is loyalty rather than perfidy that brings down the enterprise.

Honour among thieves is also a key to *The Killing* (1956), which is justly celebrated for its intricate, non-linear narrative. As directed by Stanley Kubrick, *The Killing* features laconic performances by most of its protagonists balanced against a hysterical undertone in the work of Elisha Cook Jr. and Timothy Carey. Kubrick's penchant for fatalistic plots meshes perfectly with the double-cross and clipped

Publicity still for 'Criss Cross' (1949)
Steve Thompson (Burt Lancaster) will do anything to stay near ex-wife Anna (Yvonne De Carlo). This includes helping Anna's new husband Slim Dundee steal from Steve's armoured car.

'Everything is determined, the beginning as well as the end, by forces over which we have no control. It is determined for the insect as well as the star. Human beings, vegetables, or cosmic dust, we all dance to a mysterious tune, intoned in the distance by an invisible piper.'

Albert Einstein [8]

65

"A man eats an apple and gets a piece of the core stuck between his teeth, you know. He tries to work it out with some cellophane from a cigarette pack. What happens? The cellophane gets stuck in there, too. What was the use? I knew, one way or the other, I'd end up seeing Anna that night."

Steve Thompson (Burt Lancaster) in *Criss Cross* (1949)

RIGHT
Still from 'Criss Cross' (1949)
During the robbery, Slim double-crosses Steve by murdering Steve's partner and then trying to kill Steve. Steve is shot but he manages to kill two of the gang and is lauded as a hero.

BELOW
On the set of 'Criss Cross' (1949)
To film Steve driving the security van, an image of the background is projected onto a screen behind the van, and light is shone through the rotating wood and perplex on the left so that dappled shadows appear on the van. This, combined with a gentle rocking of the van, gives the impression of movement.

"I hadn't realized those old gloomy movies and novels were gloomy at all. They were stylish, effective, hot-stuff... God knows how the noir coloration came to be. It was in the air, the politics, chiefly Hemingway, Hammett and Chandler, as you suggest. We enjoyed them and the existentialism, too. So I think film noir was actually not noir at all but 'la vie en rose.'"

Screenwriter Daniel Fuchs on *Criss Cross* (1949) [9]

LEFT
Still from 'Criss Cross' (1949)
Steve finds Anna with the money from the heist, but before she can leave Slim Dundee (Dan Duryea) finds them and shoots them dead. The film begins and ends with them in each other's arms, giving a tragic dimension to this compelling film.

BELOW
On the set of 'Criss Cross' (1949)
Director Robert Siodmak (centre) goes through a scene with Yvonne De Carlo and Burt Lancaster.

immune to infighting and antagonism within their ranks. One of the last classic-period examples, *Odds Against Tomorrow* (1959), uses racial animus to create that conflict. More typical are characters like Slim Dundee and Steve Thompson in *Criss Cross*, reluctant partners in crime brought together by a fatal woman.

After the sudden death of Mark Hellinger, his producer on *The Killers*, reworking the complex narrative of *Criss Cross* was left to Siodmak and writer Daniel Fuchs. The original setting of the robbery, which was a racetrack as in *The Killing*, was changed to an armoured car hold-up. More significantly also added, in the manner of *The Killers*, was a flashback structure and a protagonist doomed because he picks the wrong woman.

From the opening aerial shot across the darkened city and into the parking lot of a small nightclub, *Criss Cross* invokes the indicators of fatality in film noir: a distanced view of an anonymous urban landscape; the frenetic chords of Miklós Rózsa's score gradually ceding to the dance music from within the club; the preordained movement inward, drawn by an unknown object or person. As the image dissolves from an omniscient perspective to a particularized one – the headlights of a car sweep across the parking lot and illuminate two figures embracing – the deterministic quality of the narrative is effectively anticipated. This introduction of the lovers, Steve and Anna, exploits the noir conventions to plunge the viewer abruptly into their point of view and to isolate a moment that mixes fear of discovery with sexual excitement. Only through subsequent flashbacks is the true nature of Thompson's relationship to Anna detailed. His narration is almost a lament and explicitly deterministic: "From the start, it all went one way. It was in the cards or it was fate or a jinx or whatever you want to call it."

The fear and excitement so obvious in that first scene are components of Thompson's fatal obsession, which he details when he recalls his reencounter with Anna. The viewer intrudes into his reverie, alone at the bar, not dissolute but seeking escape. As Thompson tries to dispel his ill-defined disquiet, a point-of-view shot abruptly compels the audience to co-experience what he sees. Through the hazy room a long lens isolates one couple dancing. As Thompson strains for a better look, the woman turns. For a moment, her face is visible then lost again in the crowd. The woman is Anna, Thompson's former wife, with whom he is still emotionally and physically obsessed. Not only do the formal elements of the shot idealize Anna's appearance, but the use of point-of-view makes an economic, nonverbal connection between that appearance and Thompson's opinion of her. Anna is suddenly there, oneirically before him as if sprung from the depths of that initial reverie. In fact, Thompson might at first suspect that he is hallucinating since there is no reason, other than his overwhelming desire, for her to be in the nightclub. Because this articulation of the relationship between Thompson and Anna is purely visual, it cannot be misconstrued. The audience is not given a perspective that is literally what Thompson sees – the long lens and slow motion belie that. Rather the shot is a remarkable composite subjective: what Thompson sees is distorted by the powerful emotion that he feels.

ABOVE
Still from 'The Killing' (1956)
Highwaymen and outlaws have always worn
masks, and the film noir gangsters were no
exception. Here Johnny (Sterling Hayden) steals
the takings of a race track in Stanley Kubrick's
time-bending heist movie.

RIGHT
Still from 'Kansas City Confidential' (1952)
The criminals in this gang not only hide their
faces from the guards but also wear masks when
they meet, so that only the mastermind, an
embittered ex-cop, knows their true identities.

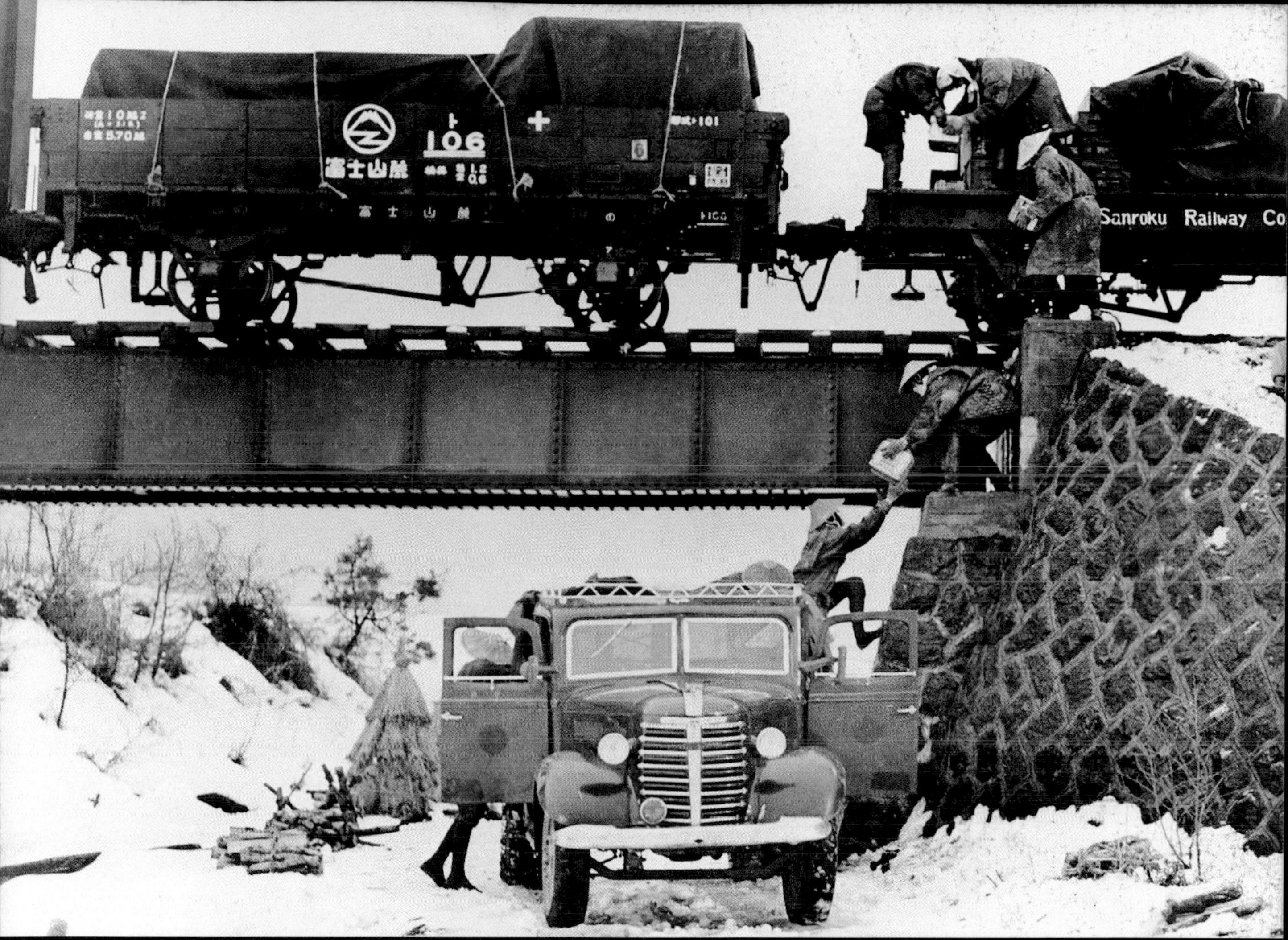

ABOVE
Still from 'House of Bamboo' (1955)
In Japan, where the film is set, the gang of American ex-soliders would be instantly recognisable, so they dress like natives.

LEFT
Still from 'Plunder Road' (1957)
The gang steal gold destined for the San Francisco mint. The gold is split on three trucks, and the film follows each attempt to get away with the gold.

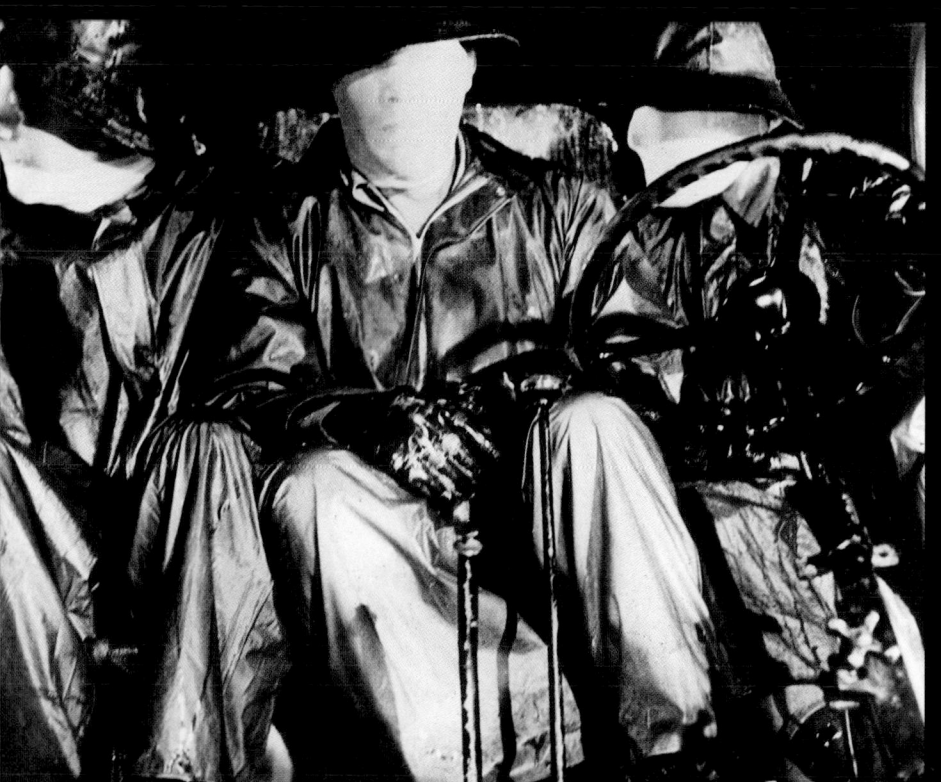

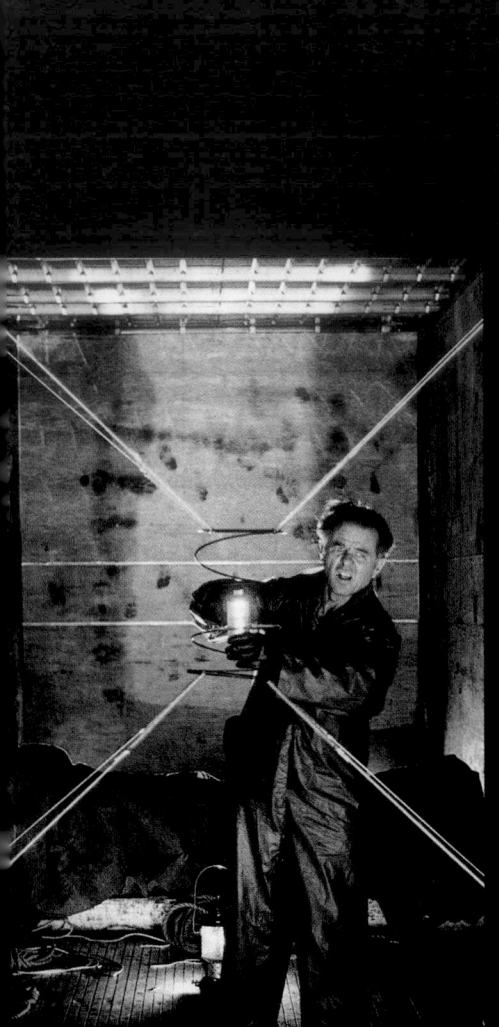

This sequence is the key to *Criss Cross* and to the ultimate destruction of its protagonist. The day-lit exteriors of Angel's Flight, where Thompson lives, his visits to Anna at Dundee's spacious home and the full-lit shots of him at work are all naturalistic in their lighting and composition. As informed by the subjective viewpoint and the voice-over of the first scenes they become functionally if not stylistically noir, for they reflect Thompson's rekindled dissatisfaction with his drab environment. The expressionistic staging of the robbery with its violence, its dark, masked figures moving apprehensively through smoke-filled frames and its deadly excitement, becomes a nightmarish variant, again from Thompson's point of view, of the sexual promise of the initial sequence. This carries over into the claustrophobic paranoia of Thompson in the hospital, where, in a new series of anxious close shots echoing the introductory ones of him, he hopes simultaneously for and against Anna's arrival. Finally, the slow pan down to Thompson's and Anna's bodies, which have fallen together in a mortal repose undisturbed by the rising blare of sirens, reverses the inward sweep of the film's first shot while Rózsa's ominous score forms a dirge-like coda.

By beginning with the dynamics of the relationship between Thompson and Anna and by establishing it precisely and particularly through the *mise en scène*, Siodmak irrevocably ties all the events that follow to that first fatal moment in the nightclub, a moment that will govern Thompson's destiny. Would it be 'in the cards' without Anna's false promises? "All those things that happened to us, everything that went before, we'll forget it," she tells Steve. "You'll see. I'll make you forget it. After it's done, after it's all over and we're safe, it'll be just you and me. You and me. The way it should've been all along from the start."

In using the flashback structure and narration, Siodmak makes it clear from the start that Anna's vision of 'you and me' is doomed. He combines the elements of mad love, heist gone wrong and emotional duplicity even more powerfully than in *The Killers* and makes *Criss Cross* one of the most tragic and compelling of noir films.

ABOVE
Still from 'Plunder Road' (1957)
The heist is so meticulously planned that it is successful. However, there is always a fatal flaw, either in the plan or in the people, that gets them caught or killed. In 'Plunder Road' Skeets (Elisha Cook, Jr.) has a freight truck full of gold but their weight gives them away at a weighing station and they are caught.

RIGHT
Still from 'The Asphalt Jungle' (1950)
When the double crosses start coming thick and fast, Dix Handley gives mastermind Doc Riedenschneider (Sam Jaffe, right) some money and tells him to run. But Doc stops to admire a young girl dance and is picked up by the police.

OPPOSITE
Still from 'Rififi' (1955)
After the nail-biting heist, a rival gang kidnap Joe the Swede's son in exchange for the loot. Here Tony le Stéphanois (Jean Servais, right) finds the boy with Rémi Grutter (Robert Hossein). Tony will eventually die to save the boy.

ABOVE
Still from 'White Heat' (1949)
When the gang is eventually hunted down, the leader often tries to climb higher. Here mother-obsessed Cody Jarrett (James Cagney) shouts "Made it Ma. Top of the world!" as he is consumed in flames during the climactic shoot-out.

LEFT
Still from 'House of Bamboo' (1955)
Gang leader Sandy Dawson (Robert Ryan) is hunted down by undercover cop Eddie Kenner in an amusement park on top of a building in Tokyo. There is a hint of homosexuality in Sandy's favouritism towards Kenner, and Kenner does some morally reprehensible things to remain as part of the gang.

ABOVE

Still from 'The Killing' (1956)

Everybody in the gang ends up either dead or in jail. George (Elisha Cook, Jr.) lies dead, free at last. He had been as trapped in life as a bird in a cage.

RIGHT

Still from 'The Killing' (1956)

George and his high-maintenance wife Sherry have a sadomasochistic relationship. When she hears that George is part of a robbery, she and her lover plan to steal the money from the robbers. The result is a massacre. The bodies litter the room like the discarded betting slips on the floor of the racetrack at the beginning of the film.

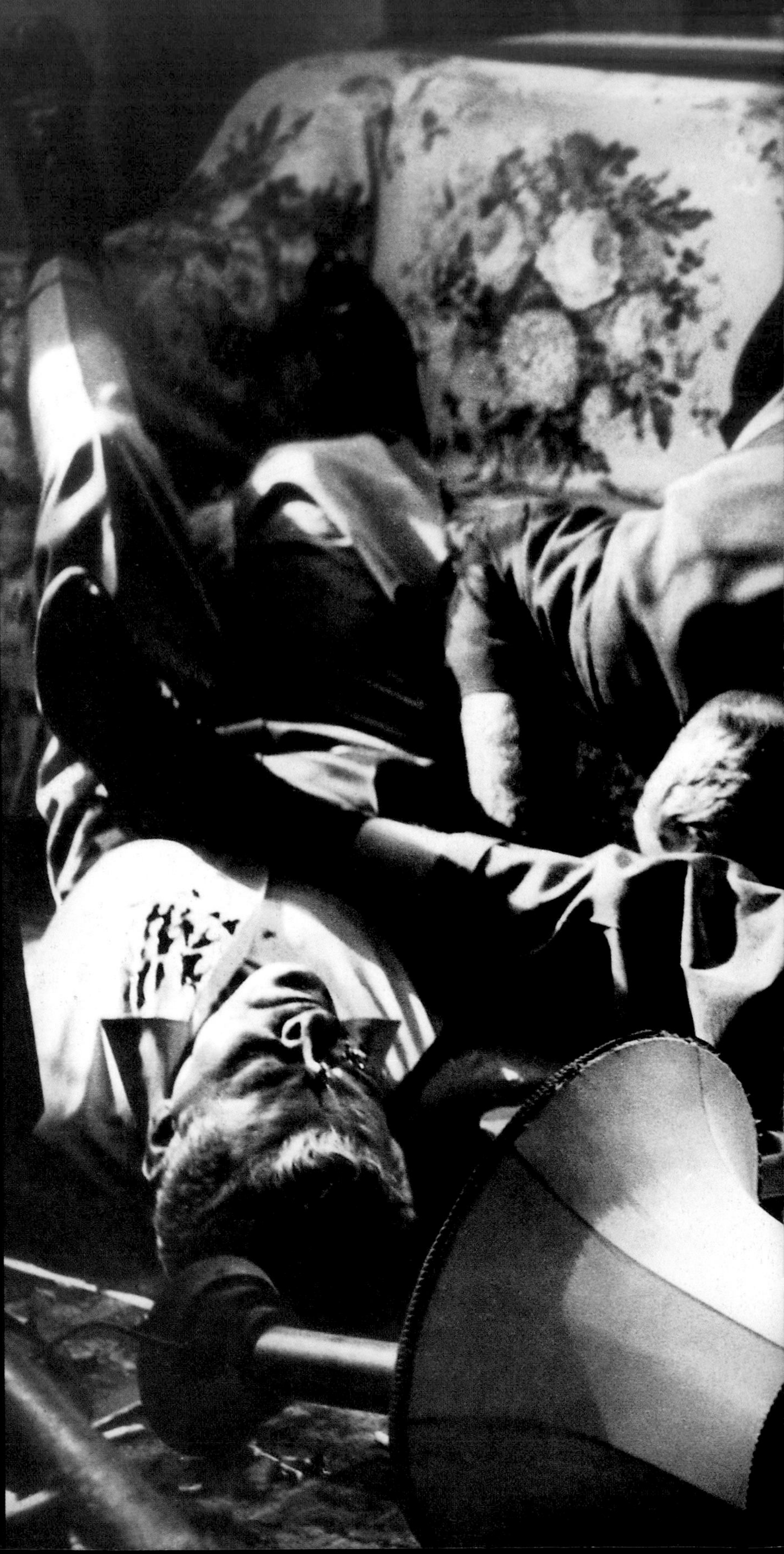

Robert Siodmak

Robert Siodmak was born in Dresden on 8 August 1904. After a course of study at the local Academy of the Three Kings (interrupted by time spent in a special school for problem students), Siodmak briefly went into acting and toured with a repertory company. Condemned by his extreme myopia and bulging eyes to low-paying character parts, Siodmak returned to Dresden and became a bank clerk. After the German economic collapse ruined the banking industry, in 1925 Siodmak got a job writing titles and editing silent films. In 1929, while working as an assistant director, Siodmak convinced his employers to fund a short film study of Berliners on their day off, *Menschen am Sonntag* (*People on Sunday*), on which his collaborators included his brother Kurt, Billy Wilder, Edgar G. Ulmer and Fred Zinnemann. The following year Siodmak was signed by UFA as a feature director. In 1933 his film *Brennendes Geheimnis* (*The Burning Secret*, 1933) was denounced by Joseph Goebbels and pulled from release. Because of his Jewish heritage Siodmak and his brother fled to Paris, where they worked in the French film industry until the German invasion of France in 1940. Although sons of an American citizen, neither of the Siodmak brothers had been to the United States before they again emigrated there. After a short stint at Paramount, which loaned him out to Twentieth Century-Fox and Republic, and his first film noir, *Fly by Night* (1942), Siodmak moved to Universal and directed *Son of Dracula* (1943). Following this brief excursion into horror, Siodmak almost single-handedly turned Universal into a film noir factory, with films like *Phantom Lady* and *Christmas Holiday* (both 1944), *The Suspect* and *The Strange Affair of Uncle Harry* (both 1945), *The Dark Mirror*, *The Killers* and *The Spiral Staircase* (all 1946). Siodmak worked again at Twentieth Century-Fox where he made *Cry of the City* (1948) and Paramount for *The File on Thelma Jordon* (1950), his last noir film. In 1952, he re-teamed with Burt Lancaster for the popular action comedy *The Crimson Pirate* (1952), which was shot on location in Europe. Siodmak remained in Europe and continued to direct feature films for German, British and American producers, including the English-language projects *Escape from East Berlin* (1962) and *Custer of the West* (1967). He died in Switzerland on 10 March 1973.

On the set of 'Criss Cross' (1949)
Robert Siodmak (left) positioning Yvonne De Carlo and Burt Lancaster. The physicality of the characters' relationship is important. Anna implies that Slim Dundee cannot satisfy her sexually in the way that Steve can, and this encourages Steve to try to get her back.

ABOVE
Still from 'The File on Thelma Jordon' (1950)
Thelma Jordon (Barbara Stanwyck) feels remorse for all the wrong she has done, so she uses a car cigarette lighter on Tony Laredo (Richard Rober) and their car plunges over a cliff. She confesses to her crimes to clear her lover/victim Cleve Marshall, but he will remain emotionally scarred for the rest of his life.

LEFT
Still from 'Phantom Lady' (1944)
When Carol Richman (Ella Raines) tries to save her boss from a death sentence, she pretends to be a good time girl and is taken to a (presumably drug-fuelled) jazz session by Cliff March (Elisha Cook, Jr.). The orgasmic intensity of the scene is one of high points of the film.

Docu-Noir

A significant influence on post-World War Two noir was the neorealist movement of the Italian cinema. Films like *Roma, città aperta* (*Rome, Open City*, 1945), *Paisà* (*Paisan*, 1946) and *Ladri di biciclette* (*The Bicycle Thief*, 1948) were released in the United States and gained admirers among critics and film-makers alike. Although many titles, such as *Ossessione* (1943), Luchino Visconti's unlicensed adaptation of *The Postman Always Rings Twice*, were not imported, many of these ground-breaking neorealist films, shot on practical locations with minimal budgets, were particularly relevant to noir, which had been most often consigned to the lower budget units of the major studios and only found welcome arms at RKO and with alternative studios such as Allied Artists or Producers Releasing Corporation. As noir films began to mix studio scenes with real locations while basing their stories on non-fiction sources like newspapers, magazines and public records, their style changed, and Italian neorealism joined German expressionism and French poetic realism in the list of affiliated film movements. *Call Northside 777* (1948) is based on a *Chicago Times* article that relates the true story of Chicago reporter, P.J. McNeal (James Stewart), who becomes an advocate for a cleaning woman whose son has been unjustly imprisoned. In *The Naked City* (1948) the narrator sums up the documentary tone of the films with his now famous line, "There are eight million stories in the naked city and this is one of them." *The Naked City*, directed by noir film-maker and subsequent blacklistee Jules Dassin and written by fellow traveller Albert Maltz, brings its own brand of social consciousness to a story based on newspaper files, set largely in the tenement neighbourhoods of New York City and partially inspired by the dark photo-journalism of Arthur Fellig aka WeeGee. In *Crossfire* (1947), director Edward Dmytryk draws on the anti-Semitic ethos present in the United States even after the recent revelations concerning the horrors of Nazi concentration camps. A Jewish man, Joseph Samuels, is beaten to death for no apparent reason. The remainder of the film is the detailed investigation of this senseless hate crime. With Jack Webb's *Dragnet* (1954), a feature version of Webb's successful foray into docu-television, the director-writer takes another story from the files of the Los Angeles Police Department ("The story you are about to see is true. Only the names have been changed to protect the innocent…") and pursues a murderer through the streets of Los Angeles, delivering his trademark deadpan expression and clipped dialogue to an audience already familiar with his TV persona.

OPPOSITE
Still from 'T-Men' (1948)
Dennis O'Brien (Dennis O'Keefe, centre) is a Treasury agent who goes undercover as a small time hood to break a counterfeiting ring. Here Dennis takes a beating when he passes fake money in an illegal gambling joint. This will get him noticed by the gang.

PAGES 82/83
On the set of 'The Naked City' (1948)
Ted de Corsica is the striding figure at the bottom of the picture. Director Jules Dassin, who is bringing traffic chaos to Delancey Street, stands on the ladder behind him. Dassin and cinematographer William Daniels, who won an Oscar for his work here, used locations to make New York City a character in the story.

'Appearance should never attain reality and if nature conquers, then must art retire.'
Friedrich Schiller

ABOVE
Still from 'The House on 92nd Street' (1945)
Hammershon (Leo G. Carroll) looks into the
mirror unaware that he is being filmed by the
F.B.I. This film established the conventions of the
docu-noir: location shooting, a stentorian
narrator, based on a real case, and director
Henry Hathaway used the real people in the real
locations when he could. This formula was
applied to other film noirs like Alfred Hitchcock's
'The Wrong Man' (1956).

RIGHT
Photo from F.B.I. files (25 June 1941)
The film still above was based on this F.B.I.
photo of Nazi fifth columnist Frederick Duquesne
(right) in the office of Harry Sawyer. The film
celebrates the F.B.I.'s surveillence techniques
(two-way mirrors, hidden microphones) and the
F.B.I. loaned some of this equipment to the
production.

ABOVE
Still from 'He Walked by Night' (1949)
Brilliant thief Ray Morgan/Roy Martin (Richard Basehart, centre), is an alienated loner who uses electronic equipment and his ingenuity to constantly thwart capture by the police.

LEFT
Still from 'He Walked by Night' (1949)
Chuck Jones (Jimmy Cardwell) and Sgt. Marty Brennan (Scott Brady) watch forensic scientist Lee (Jack Webb) handle some nitroglycerine. The film concentrates on police techniques and procedures. Jack Webb used elements of this film and combined it with his own extensive research for his 'Dragnet' radio series (1949–1956), TV series (1951–1959, 1967–1970) and films (1954, 1969).

ABOVE
Still from 'Crossfire' (1947)
Montgomery (Robert Ryan) is a racist who kills a Jew. (Interestingly, in Richard Brooks' novel the victim was homosexual.) The intensity of Robert Ryan's performance gives the film an edge and typecast him as a man full of hate. For example, he was also a racist in the heist film 'Odds Against Tomorrow' (1959).

RIGHT
Still from 'Crossfire' (1947)
Montgomery is a hunted man, as were the film-makers. Producer Adrian Scott and director Edward Dmytryk were two of the Hollywood Ten jailed by the House Un-American Activities Committee for their Communist activities.

On the set of 'Thieves' Highway' (1949)
The story of a war veteran trying to make a living by transporting produce was shot on location in San Francisco (pictured), Oakland, Highway 99, Sebastopol, Calistoga, Santa Rosa, Hueneme and Oxnard, California. The film shows that the industry is run by liars, thieves and murderers.

T-Men, directed by Anthony Mann and photographed by John Alton, who are among noir's most prestigious directors and cameramen, also draws its story from actual case files, in this instance those of the Treasury Department. Like *The Naked City* and *Dragnet*, it also uses a narrator. His stentorian voice leads the viewer through the convoluted plot of the film to its convenient patriotic resolution. In order to establish its credentials the movie even introduces a former chief in the Treasury Department, who sits stiffly behind a desk and drones on in monotone about the work of Treasury agents. The film also has its share of locations, many in Los Angeles, intermixed with studio scenes. The film-makers are obviously intent on establishing a neorealist tone with the audience before plunging into the sordid story they are about to tell. It is almost as if they are afraid the audience will not believe their plot unless they back it up with documentary style footage, a 'voice of God' narrator and real government officials.

What obviously interested Mann in this project is the same theme that dominates so many of his films from *Raw Deal* (1948) to *Devil's Doorway* (1950), *The Man from Laramie* (1955), *Men in War* (1957) and *El Cid* (1961): not its basis in reality, but the psychology of its main character. In this case Dennis O'Brien (Dennis O'Keefe) is a Treasury agent or 'T-Man' brought in, along with his partner Tony Genaro, first to infiltrate a Detroit mob and then later a Los Angeles

ABOVE
Still from 'The Lawless' (1950)
The docu-noir was often used to present a social conscience to its audience. In 'The Lawess', when a Mexican fruitpicker hits a cop, a town explodes into lawlessness and racial prejudice.

LEFT
Still from 'The Phenix City Story' (1955)
A lawyer returns from the war to find his home town a den of corruption.

Still from 'T-Men' (1948)
Moxie (Charles McGraw, left) gives Dennis a beating, whilst henchman Brownie (Jack Overman) looks on. The high level of sudden and fatal violence in the film keeps the viewer on their toes. Surprisingly, the undercover agents seem to fit in very well with their dark surroundings.

"T-Men was really my first film.... The film was the first 'documentary' of that genre and did extremely well for a 'B-unit' production. I was fairly satisfied with certain sequences: the murder of Wallace Ford in the steam bath, for example, or the beating of Dennis O'Keefe."

Director Anthony Mann [10]

gang in order to expose a countrywide counterfeiting ring. One of Mann's main themes has always been suffering and violence. His male protagonists endure torturous conditions and do it almost poetically, reinforced by the exquisitely claustrophobic photography he favours, particularly in his noir films. *T-Men* is no exception. In fact, the chiaroscuro lighting and the metaphorical qualities of O'Brien's descent create even more tension in the film, as documentary 'realism' and expressionistic symbolism clash within the first ten minutes of the story.

Mann's fondness for exploring the themes of violence as well as the psychology of his characters while creating a vividly expressionistic atmosphere can be seen throughout the movie. In an early scene O'Brien is beaten brutally in a dingy bathroom by a large group of men who caught him passing counterfeit bills. This is part of his ruse to establish his credibility with Schemer, one of the keys to bringing down the Los Angeles mob. As he is thrown out into the alley, he rolls towards the camera and smiles. This smile can be read in several ways. It could be a smile of triumph in that his cover as a counterfeiter is assured; but there is also an element of masochism in it. At a later time he is tortured by Moxie, a thug working for the mob whom the audience had seen in the early part of the movie murdering an informant before a storage tank in downtown L.A.

O'Brien endures and so is taken to one of the mob bosses, Shiv, who has called
O'Brien's former boss Vantucci in Detroit to check his 'credentials.'

Mann furthers establishes the metaphorical dimensions of the film by setting a
series of scenes in steam baths. These are Schemer's favourite haunts. So they are
where O'Brien goes in order to first find and then track him. In these steam-filled
rooms crowded with sweating half-naked men, whose faces register more
discomfort than pleasure, Mann intensifies the hellish quality of O'Brien's journey
through the use of diffused, almost luminous lighting. It is appropriate that Schemer
finally meets his end in one of these circles of hell as Moxie, on orders from the mob
bosses whom Schemer has threatened to expose in order to protect himself, locks
Schemer inside and turns up the steam. The terrified Schemer beats on the window
of the door and flails around like a trapped animal before collapsing onto the floor.

One of the most striking elements of this movie is how easily O'Brien, and to a
lesser degree Genaro, fits into this underworld of violence and corruption. Since we
have seen very little of O'Brien before he becomes Hannigan, the mobster, and since
all we see of him at the end is a photo in a magazine of him recovering from his
gunshot wounds, received while chasing and then dispatching Moxie, the viewer's
sympathies with this character are of necessity muted. He speaks with the tough,
hardbitten diction of a hood, dresses in flashy suits and participates in acts of

Still from 'T-Men' (1948)
Dennis' partner Tony Genaro (Alfred Ryder, right)
is uncovered as a T-man, so Moxie kills him with
Dennis having to watch and unable to help. The
film was based on real U.S. Treasury Department
cases.

violence without any noticeable qualms. The only moment in which we see O'Brien affected by a brutal act is when his own partner is exposed as a T-Man and murdered by Moxie. O'Brien does nothing to save his friend, not wanting to risk blowing his own cover and the government's case against this counterfeiting ring. It is an indicator of how far he has sunk into this world of callousness and brutality that he is able to witness such an act and restrain himself. Even the pompous narrator seems to point out the irony of O'Brien watching his friend die for 'a scrap of paper' which tells him the location of Schemer's incriminating code book.

The final scene on the freighter in L.A. harbour is particularly tense and violent. O'Brien is under suspicion again and is brought by Moxie and Brownie to the top bosses of the ring in order to verify that the counterfeit plates he has are not recognizable. Eventually Miller, the photographic expert, vouches for the plates while O'Brien waits in agony, knowing he will be murdered if they are recognized. Meanwhile a group of agents have been tipped off and are on their way to the freighter to arrest the counterfeiters. When they arrive tear-gas canisters are shot onto the freighter and O'Brien pursues Moxie in a chase throughout the freighter. O'Brien is shot in the stomach but continues forward, bleeding profusely as he does. He kills Moxie and falls onto the deck of the ship. The ring is broken up and O'Brien is hailed a hero by the narrator to the chords of patriotic music. But the irony is not lost on the audience as the camera pans to a photo of the murdered Genaro in the same magazine which features O'Brien's 'heroic' story. No palliatives can relieve the unsettling after-effect of this squalid and brutal journey into urban noir.

Anthony Mann

Anthony Mann is one of the most important figures of the noir movement. Mann was born Emil Anton Bundmann on 30 June 1906 in San Diego, California. At an early age Mann began acting in local theatres and then off-Broadway after the family moved to New York in 1917. After the death of his teacher father, the young Mann quit high school to work in a factory to support his family. He continued to pursue his acting career, often working both day and night. He eventually became a director on Broadway in the 1930s. In 1938, he left the theatre, lured back to Southern California to work in Hollywood. He worked as a casting director and talent scout for the Selznick Company, where he directed screen tests for *Gone with the Wind* (1939) and *Rebecca* (1940). At Paramount he was an assistant director on *Sullivan's Travels* (1941) for Preston Sturges, who advised him that "It's better to have done something bad than to have done nothing." He began his own film directing career with low budget noirs. In the early 1940s he was producing minor noir classics like *Dr Broadway* (1942) and *The Great Flammarion* (1945) starring Erich Von Stroheim. He continued making classics like *Desperate* (1947), *Railroaded* (1947), *Raw Deal* (1948), *Follow Me Quietly*, *He Walked by Night* (both uncredited, 1949), *The Black Book* (1949), *Side Street* and *Devil's Doorway* (both 1950), often photographed by his frequent collaborator John Alton. In 1950 he began a series of noirish Westerns starring James Stewart, including *Winchester '73* (1950), *The Naked Spur* (1953) and *The Man from Laramie* (1955). He also began producing his own movies, most notably the brutal anti-war movie, *Men in War* (1957). In the 1960s, he left the United States to work on large budget European epics such as *El Cid* (1961) and *The Fall of the Roman Empire* (1964). Mann died on 29 April 1967 in the middle of his final movie, *A Dandy in Aspic*.

On the set of 'Raw Deal' (1948)
Marsha Hunt is coached by Anthony Mann. Mann was known as a director who listened to actors and who often showed the darker motivations of his characters through faces and actions rather than dialogue.

ABOVE
Still from 'Raw Deal' (1948)
Do-gooder Ann Martin (Marsha Hunt) is kidnapped by Joe Sullivan and eventually kills Fantail (John Ireland) to protect him. Joe feels guilty about introducing her to the noir world and then tries to get her out of it.

LEFT
Still from 'Follow Me Quietly' (1949)
Based on a story by Francis Rosenwald and Anthony Mann, and partially directed by Mann, this film has a sequence where the obsessed detective Grant (William Lundigan) sits and talks to a faceless mannequin constructed to look like the anonymous killer he seeks. The mannequin then turns into the killer.

On the set of 'Side Street' (1950)
Anthony Mann (right, under light) filming Cathy
O'Donnell comfort Farley Granger in the final
scene, shot on the corner of Broad Street and
Wall Street in New York City on 1 May 1949.

Love on the Run

The epitome of what Luis Buñuel calls *amour fou* or mad love has most often been associated with couples on the run not merely in film noir but as regards motion pictures in general. These fugitive couples were outcasts and outlaws, hunted and hopeless, and usually dead or dying at the film's end. As a sub-type, the fugitive couple film has a long history from D.W. Griffith's *Scarlet Days* (1919) to *Mad Love* (1995) and *Yellowknife* (2002). But even allowing for such modern variants as *Thelma and Louise* (1991), there are still only a score or two of pictures that fit this type. Many if not most of these were made as part of the era of film noir, in a fifteen-year span from *You Only Live Once* (1937) to *Where Danger Lives* (1950). Both the obsessive character of *amour fou* and the alienated posture of the fugitives in relation to society are prototypical noir themes.

In his survey of noir, 'Paint It Black', Raymond Durgnat gives a thumbnail sketch of the fugitive couples under the heading 'On the Run': 'Here the criminals, or the framed innocents are essentially passive and fugitive, and, even if tragically or despicably guilty, sufficiently sympathetic for the audience to be caught between, on the one hand, pity, identification and regret, and, on the other, moral condemnation and conformist fatalism.' Durgnat's prose is so densely packed that it masks the shortcomings of his analysis. What permits, even compels, viewer pity or identification with the innocent and guilty is the nature of most fugitive couples and their mad love: obsessive, erotically charged, far beyond simple Romanticism.

Since film noir is as much a style as it is a genre, the manner in which the wild passion of the fugitives is portrayed is more significant than the plot points that keep them on the run. Some of these lovers are little more than children, like Bowie and Keechie in Nicholas Ray's *They Live by Night* (1948). In their naiveté, typified by Keechie's request to Bowie to teach her how to kiss, this film recalls Fritz Lang's seminal couple in *You Only Live Once*.

Lang's narrative focus in that picture is typical of his deterministic world view and, like his earlier *Fury* (1936), is as concerned with the outrage of the unjustly punished as with the fugitive couple. The director's naturalistic staging relies on the conventions of casting and the innate audience sympathy for the stars, Henry Fonda as Eddie and Sylvia Sidney as Jo, to maintain identification with a fugitive couple irrevocably at odds with the forces of law and order. Lang employs a series of elegiac details to establish Eddie and Jo's romantic dependence on each other. For example,

Still from 'Gun Crazy' (1950)
Laurie Starr (Peggy Cummins): "I'm yours and I'm real."
Bart Tare (John Dall): "You're the only thing that is, Laurie. The rest is a nightmare."

"Mad love isolates the lovers, makes them ignore normal social obligations, ruptures ordinary family ties, and ultimately brings them to destruction. This love frightens society, shocks it profoundly. And society uses all its means to separate these lovers as it would two dogs in the street."

Luis Buñuel [11]

as they stand in the evening by the frog pond of a small motel, Eddie explains to Jo that the frogs mate for life and always die together. Even as they feel secure in themselves, the motel manager is inside searching through his collection of pulp detective magazines under the harsh glare of his desk lamp. When he finds several photos and a story on Eddie's criminal past, Lang underscores the irony first with a shot of a frog jumping into the pond and diffracting Eddie's reflection in the water. Then there is a view of a dark, vaporous swamp where the truck that could prove Eddie innocent of a crime of which he is not yet aware sinks into the quicksand. Although the frog pond scene could have either ridiculed the naiveté of Lang's characters or awkwardly stressed their lowly social status, Lang's staging and cutting makes it a simple, evocative metaphor for the entire narrative. As with Fonda's optimism, this moment is also a stylistic prototype for the treatment of a young and innocent couple on the run that endured throughout the noir cycle.

They Live by Night shares the elegiac aspect with You Only Live Once that almost makes Nicholas Ray's film into something of a fable. Its characters with their odd-sounding names – Bowie, Keechie, T-Dub, Chickamaw – exist in a world of grubby garages and cheap motels, cut off from the mainstream, from the ordinary, in an aura of myth. As its fugitive lovers are barely past adolescence, the key irony of They Live by Night is the very youth and innocence of its 'outlaw' protagonists. Bowie is too naive to survive because his lack of sophistication permits real criminals like T-Dub and Chickamaw to take advantage of him. How else could they persuade Bowie that the only way to clear himself of an old criminal charge is to get money for a lawyer; and how else to get money for a lawyer than by helping his friends to rob a bank? Even Keechie's common sense cannot save Bowie from his own ingenuousness. She may help by removing him from the influence of T-Dub and Chickamaw, but the couple cannot remove themselves from the deadly constraints of society itself. Like the doorbell of the wedding broker that plays an off-key wedding march, while he hawks a "deluxe ceremony including a snapshot of the happy couple," the real world touches them with its cheapness and insensitivity. It entices them with the hope of escape like the bungalow of a backwoods motel where they find temporary refuge. In the end, Bowie is guilty and he must die. But unlike Lang's treatment of Eddie Taylor, in Ray's hands, Bowie's fate seems less a question of implacable destiny than simple mischance. It could be argued that the poignancy of the relationships in both You Only Live Once and They Live by Night are as much romantic as noir. What is dark about these movies, particularly in the context of mainstream Hollywood, is that one or both halves of each couple perish. Obviously the straightforward concept of moral retribution, that the guilty must die, is at work both as an abstract dramatic element and as a requirement dictated by the Hollywood production code. The film-makers' emphasis on the innocence of their protagonists – literally for Eddie who is not guilty of the particular crime for which he is condemned and emotionally for Bowie who is ensnared by the older, duplicitous criminals – makes these films even darker and firmly imbeds them in the noir cycle.

There are more 'upbeat' examples of the fugitive couple plot in film noir. The Douglas Sirk/Sam Fuller Shockproof (1949) or Tomorrow is Another Day (1951, directed by Felix Feist, the scenarist/director of the manic 1947 The Devil Thumbs a Ride) are both examples where the fugitive couples survive; but the noir sensibility of these pictures is sustained through amour fou. Like You Only Live Once, both feature protagonists who have already been convicted of a crime when the narrative

On the set of 'You Only Live Once' (1937)
Three-time loser Eddie Taylor (Henry Fonda, left) makes his escape from prison after being wrongly arrested, tried and sentenced to death. As with 'Fury' (1936) director Fritz Lang (to right of camera in white) concentrates on the outrage of the unjustly punished.

ABOVE
On the set of 'They Live by Night' (1948)
A helicopter was used to shoot various sequences in the film. Here Chickamaw (Howard Da Silva) and T-Dub (Jay C. Flippen) are running from the cops in the opening sequence.

RIGHT
Still from 'They Live by Night' (1948)
T-Dub (back), Bowie (Farley Granger, left) and Chickamaw (right) hole up in a shack owned by Chickamaw's brother. Here, T-Dub, Bowie and Keechie (Cathy O'Donnell) listen to Chickamaw read out a short account of their escape from the prison farm.

opens. *Shockproof* adds the element of the 'rogue cop' in the parole officer whose obsessive love drives him to flee with a female parolee accused of murder. *Tomorrow is Another Day* goes even farther. The prospective couple are a bizarre mixture of innocence and depravity. The man, Bill (Steve Cochran), has grown up in prison convicted for a murder committed under the influence of an uncontrollable temper while still a youth. Paroled as an adult, he is sexually inexperienced. As portrayed by Cochran, better known for such supporting roles as the gangster who cuckolds Cagney's Cody Jarrett in *White Heat*, Bill has a physical maturity which belies his stunted emotional growth. The woman, Catherine (Ruth Roman), who becomes the object of Bill's obsessive love is a taxi dancer/prostitute. Again the element of the rogue cop is introduced, this time when a detective, who is himself in love with the woman, sexually assaults her and is killed. Like most of Hollywood's fugitive couples, including Eddie and Jo and Bowie and Keechie, the lovers of *Tomorrow is Another Day* are proletarian. As with the couple in *Shockproof*, who find work in an oil field, Bill and Catherine seek refuge in the anonymity of migrant farming. In the end the subtlest irony of both *Shockproof* and *Tomorrow is Another Day* is that neither of these couples take charge of their own destiny and create their own salvation. Rather they survive because they happen to be exonerated. For many fugitive couples, particularly in the context of film noir, the emotional sustenance

Still from 'They Live by Night' (1948)
After the robbery and subsequent car crash, Keechie tends to Bowie's injured back. In this tender scene, the youngsters somehow manage to let each other know that they care for each other. Director Nicholas Ray punctuates these intimate moments with scenes of unusual violence that add poignancy to the doomed love.

ABOVE
Still from 'Where Danger Lives' (1950)
Dr. Jeff Cameron (Robert Mitchum) treats Margo Lannington (Faith Domergue) after an attempted suicide and then falls for the girl. In this picture he begins to suspect that she is psychotic. And his diagnosis is correct.

RIGHT
Still from 'Shockproof' (1949)
Parole officer Griff Marat (Cornel Wilde) falls for and then marries his parolee Jenny Marsh (Patricia Knight). After she becomes embroiled in a shooting they must go on the run.

which may be derived from any hope of escape or the kindness of strangers is secondary to their own obsessive love. When *amour fou* is, as Buñuel suggested, an all-consuming passion, every action from hiding out to stealing money to killing interlopers is a desperate attempt to remain at large where that passion may be sustained.

"We go together. I don't know how. Maybe like guns and ammunition go together."

Bart Tare, *Gun Crazy* (1950)

Although it was made just two years later, *Gun Crazy* and its couple are far-removed from the innocence of *They Live by Night*. When Clyde first shows Bonnie his gun in Arthur Penn's *Bonnie and Clyde* (1967), she casually fondles the barrel. As a sexual metaphor, such a staging pales in comparison to the meeting of the lovers in director Joseph H. Lewis' *Gun Crazy*. The first shot of Annie Laurie Starr, the sideshow sharpshooter of *Gun Crazy* (originally released as *Deadly is the Female*), is from a low angle as she strides into the frame firing two pistols above her head. Bart Tare accepts her open challenge to a shoot-off with anyone in the audience; and soon he and Laurie are firing at crowns of matches on each other's head. The sequence ends with an exchange of glances between the two. Laurie, the loser, smiles seductively. Bart, the victor with his potency established, grins from ear to ear.

This is merely the first meeting. Bart gets a job with the carnival and from then on Laurie wears her beret at an angle, her sweaters tight and her lipstick thick. After a jealous sideshow manager fires them both, they live the high life until Bart's money runs out. Laurie tries to convince Bart that there is more money to be had by staging shooting exhibitions in banks rather than tents. When he hesitates, she sits on the edge of a bed, demurely slips on her stockings and issues her ultimatum: take it or leave me. Bart capitulates.

The aura of eroticism that Lewis builds so intensely into the first part of *Gun Crazy* is, albeit 1950 vintage, anything but subtle. As Borde and Chaumeton enthusiastically noted back in 1955, '*Gun Crazy*, we dare say, brought an exceptionally attractive but murderous couple to the screen.' The physical aspect of the lovers does much to influence the viewer's perception; and the performance of the actors can sustain or counteract the visual impression, often assisted by the physical details of costuming and make-up.

Because they are an attractive couple and because, as Bart puts it, they go together explosively like guns and ammunition, the intensity of the budding *amour fou* of the couple in *Gun Crazy* is immediate and overt. His companions on the carnival outing cannot help but sense it, as does the sideshow manager, who hires Bart nonetheless. While Laurie's passion is less obvious at first, she not only marries Bart but pins her hopes on him. At that point, the full madness of *amour fou* is ready to erupt.

As *Gun Crazy* progresses the lovers' continued physical attraction is keyed, for Laurie at least, to the excitement of their crime spree. Laurie tells Bart that she gets afraid and that is why she almost shoots down innocent people. Her real feelings are most clear in the celebrated long take during a bank robbery in the small town of Hampton. With the camera in the back of the stolen Cadillac for the entire sequence, Bart and Laurie drive into town dressed in Western costumes, ostensibly to be part of a passing carnival. The suggestion, of course, is that they are

"I called the entire crew in to explain what I wanted to do: 'I'd like to start with a sign which says 'Welcome to Hampton' about a mile out of town. Then we go through town; have the boy and the girl talking; have them go in; hold up the bank; have her encounter a policeman on the street; do some talking; knock the policeman out; get into the car; drive away with the hold-up money; and get out of town, with a sign 'You Are Now Leaving Hampton,' another mile away. With all the dialogue that's in the script, I want to do this in one take.'

"The front of the Cadillac we used was the same, but it was a stretched-out model, it was one of those extra rear seats for conveying a lot of people. They cleared all the seats out. The sound man sat in the back with portable equipment. There were two 2x12 plywood boards across the entire the back of this station wagon or bus. And these were greased boards and a camera head was put on them with a jockey saddle, and the camera operator sat in the saddle and when they dollied they merely slid him along the greased silent boards. Strapped to the top of the vehicle were two sound men with microphones, and inside the car were little button microphones which would pick-up all the sounds. And we went through that town, and before we made the shot I turned to Peggy [Cummins] and John [Dall] and said, 'Now look, you know the intent of this scene. I have no dialogue for it because none can be written, except those words that have to be spoken to the policeman, those are set. But the dialogue that you will supply is what you see. You're coming into a strange town, if there are people in the way, you'll refer to that.' Well these two kids were marvelous. We made it one take; and we were through at ten o'clock in the morning."

Director Joseph H. Lewis on the Hampton Robbery sequence in *Gun Crazy* (1950) [12]

Still from 'Gun Crazy' (1950)
Laurie is sexually aroused by gunplay, whereas Bart loves the aesthetic beauty of guns and their precision. When Laurie turns to shoot a bank guard, Bart stops her because he doesn't understand why they should kill another living thing just so that they can live without working.

Still from 'Gun Crazy' (1950)

Bart caresses his guns whilst Laurie dresses provocatively. You get the impression that sex is always better after a bank job. In this scene Bart wants to stop their life of crime because he knows it will escalate into murder, but Laurie makes it clear that she wants action.

"It was as if the gun was something he had to have. The way other boys have to have jack-knives or harmonicas or baseball bats."

Miss Wynn (Virginia Farmer) in *Gun Crazy* (1950)

throwbacks to another era, desperadoes of an ilk closer to Jesse James or Belle Starr than Bonnie and Clyde. While Bart is inside the bank, Laurie uses her charms to distract and knock out a policeman who happens by. The encounter has agitated and thrilled her. As they race off, she looks back, her hands around Bart's neck as if to embrace him. In that sustained, breathless glance, backwards towards the camera, her smile is unmistakably sexual.

By more contemporary standards, the mere innuendo of sexual pleasure from a criminal act may seem rather tame. But the staging of the scene in *Gun Crazy*, the tightly controlled perspective from the back of the car and the entire sequence shot without a cut, creates a tension for the viewer that is subtly analogous to the couple's. The release of the tension as the sequence ends is keyed to Laurie's expression. What is building, to use more contemporary terminology, is an addiction. Laurie's addiction to violence, initially motivated by the desire for "money and all the things it will buy," is now the need for an adrenaline rush. In feeding her habit, Bart is a typical codependent.

Unlike earlier fugitive couples, who flee to save themselves from unjust accusations, Bart and Laurie choose to become criminals. As they come to depend more and more on each other, the process of *They Live by Night* is reversed. Rather than being innocents whose total, platonic interdependence becomes a sexual

relationship, Bart and Laurie's purely physical attraction becomes an emotional connection.

Appropriately then, the emotional climax of the picture follows immediately after their last job together. Laurie had planned for them to separate and rejoin later to throw off any pursuers. They drive to a second car and start off in opposite directions. Abruptly and at the same moment, they veer around and rejoin each other. Like Buñuel's archetypes, Lewis' couple stand embracing in the street and figuratively serve notice on society that they will not be separated. After this declaration of *amour fou*, that they will perish is a given. They die together, he shooting her in a last, perverse act of love.

Still from 'Gun Crazy' (1950)
When they work together at the carnival, their boss Packett says that they are "like a pair of wild animals." At the end, they are hunted down like animals and trapped. Bart does not want any more killing (in these same hills, as a boy he once had a deer in his sights but could not shoot) and so he shoots Laurie dead. The gunfire triggers the police guns and Bart drops down dead with Laurie.

"She ain't the type that makes a happy home. It's just that some guys are born smart about women and some guys are born dumb. You were born dumb."

Bluey-Bluey the clown (Stanley Prager) in *Gun Crazy* (1950)

Joseph H. Lewis

On the set of 'The Undercover Man' (1949)
Joseph H. Lewis (in white hat under camera) watches Glenn Ford (left) go through his paces. Although this docu-noir was set in Chicago and Lewis did his meticulous research in Chicago, the whole film was shot on the back lot in Los Angeles.

Joseph H. Lewis was born in New York City on 6 April 1907. He went West in the early 1930s and with the assistance of his older brother Ben, who had started as an editor in the silent era, Lewis moved from office and camera assistant at MGM to editing serials for Mascot Pictures (which soon merged with Monogram and Consolidated to form Republic Pictures). Lewis graduated to directing B-Westerns on *Courage of the West* (1937) at Universal. He continued to direct Westerns well into the 1960s on such television shows as *The Rifleman, Bonanza* and *The Big Valley*. He acquired the nickname 'Wagon Wheel Joe,' because he would often frame shots through the spokes of a wagon wheel, which raised complaints from the editors at Universal who had trouble cutting into his master scenes. In the early 1940s, Lewis branched out into the Bowery Boys series, some low-budget horror films and salacious PRC titles such as *Secrets of a Co-Ed* (1942). After a brief stint in the armed forces, Lewis directed one of the Falcon series at RKO and was signed by Columbia to a 12-day shoot of *My Name is Julia Ross* (1945). It took Lewis 18 to 20 days to complete the picture, but against all odds it was a considerable success as a top-billed, A-level release. Alternating between independent productions and studios B-movies, a distinctive string of noir films followed: *So Dark the Night* (1946), *The*

Undercover Man (1949), *A Lady Without Passport* (1950), *Desperate Search* (1952), *Cry of the Hunted* (1953) and *The Big Combo* (1955), the latter ranking with *Gun Crazy* as a major contribution to the noir cycle. Lewis returned briefly to Westerns with *A Lawless Street* (1955) and the unusual revenge story *Terror in a Texas Town* (1958). He finished his career working in television, the residuals from which he often credited for sustaining him comfortably during his long retirement living aboard his ship from the late 1960s until his death at age 93 in Marina del Rey, California on 30 August 2000.

Still from 'My Name is Julia Ross' (1945)
Julia Ross (Nina Foch) thought she had landed on her feet when she got a post as a personal secretary, but when she wakes up from a drugged sleep she finds herself trapped in a house, supposedly somebody's mad wife. Who will believe that she is Julia Ross?

Male Violence

Noir has always been an effective vehicle for exploring the ethos of violence, particularly male violence. In Jim Thompson's seminal novel *The Killer Inside Me* (1952), filmed by Burt Kennedy in 1975, Lou Ford is a respected peace officer on the outside but on the inside he is a cold-blooded murderer painfully aware of his own demons: 'I'll never be free as long as I live…' Ford leads a double life, much like the actor Anthony John (Ronald Colman) in the aptly titled *A Double Life* (1948). John receives the accolades of his audiences for his performance as Othello while nightly he struggles with his own murderous jealousy towards both his estranged wife and his lover. In *On Dangerous Ground* (1952), directed by Nicholas Ray, who also directed *In a Lonely Place*, decorated city cop Jim Wilson (Robert Ryan) finds himself sinking into a pattern of abuse not only towards the suspects he encounters in his work but towards everyone around him. In *Hangover Square* (1945) Laird Cregar plays a sensitive composer who lapses into schizophrenia and becomes a brutal serial killer. Raymond Chandler's screenplay for the movie *The Blue Dahlia* (1946) sees dedicated friend and decorated war veteran Buzz (William Bendix) experiencing blackouts and fits of murderous rage that make him the chief murder suspect. Even his tenderness towards his buddies cannot hide the violence, which is ready to erupt at any moment. In Fritz Lang's *The Big Heat* (1953) Detective Dave Bannion (Glenn Ford) goes on a personal vendetta after the death of his wife in a car bombing. Even though he returns to the arms of the legitimate police force at the end of the movie, this in no way mitigates the violence he commits as well as instigates against those he believes guilty.

In a Lonely Place (1950) revolves around a respected and successful screenwriter who, although admittedly in a creative slump, still lives the glamorous Hollywood life of celebrity nightclubs, expensive cars, stylish Spanish stucco flats and wannabe actresses who are more than willing to come home with him. But Dixon Steele has his demons too. The film-makers expose these character flaws to the audience very early in the movie, as Steele pulls up to a stop in his car and is hailed by a young actress. Her older husband becomes upset and demands that Dixon stop flirting with his wife. Steele calls him "a pig" and gets out of the car to fight him. The man speeds off in fear. Lest the audience think this an isolated incident, the film-makers create another similar encounter in Steele's favourite nightclub where he meets his agent Mel with Barnes, a director who wants Steele to adapt a tawdry romance

Publicity still for 'White Heat' (1949)
Cody Jarrett (James Cagney) is the epitome of not so repressed male rage.

'Methought I heard a voice cry 'Sleep no more!
Macbeth does murder sleep,' the innocent sleep,
Sleep that knits up the ravell'd sleeve of care,
The death of each day's life …'

William Shakespeare, *Macbeth*

ABOVE
Still from 'Noose' (1948)
Violent gangsters were featured in British films
like 'Brighton Rock', 'Night and the City' and
'Noose'. Americans, like crime boss Sugiani
(Joseph Calleia, foreground), were included so
that the film would succeed in America.

RIGHT
Still from 'Underworld' (1927)
Under Josef von Sternberg's stylized direction,
and with writer Ben Hecht's authentic mixture of
violence and humour, this was the first film to
use criminals as the central characters.

OPPOSITE
Still from 'High Sierra' (1941)
Roy Earle (Humphrey Bogart) marks the turning
point when gangster films became psychological.

PAGES 114/115
Still from 'The Sniper' (1952)
It was not uncommon for film noirs to be told
from the point of view of psychos like Eddie
Miller (Arthur Franz).

novel into a screenplay, and his perennially drunk actor friend Waterman (based loosely on John Barrymore). The informal meeting with Barnes enrages Steele once again as he calls the director a "popcorn salesman" for even wanting to adapt this trashy novel and eventually punches him for insulting his drunk friend.

But the most revealing moment is the scene with an old flame who is trying to smooth things over with him. He is abusive to her as well. As she is about to leave, she turns to him and asks pointedly, "Do you look down on all women or just the ones you know?" This encounter with a former lover neatly sets up the misogynistic streak in this violent man. The remainder of the film centres on the murder of a young would-be actress/hatcheck girl named Mildred, whom Steele takes home to tell him the plot to the novel he has reluctantly agreed to adapt, and the tempestuous relationship that develops between Steele and his neighbour Laurel, a witness to the events around Steele's tête-à-tête with Mildred. This theme also resonates outside the film itself. Many biographers of the director Nicholas Ray and the star Gloria Grahame, who plays Laurel, have noted that the Steele-Laurel relationship in many ways reflects the stormy affair and later marriage between Grahame and Ray.

After Mildred is found strangled and dumped in the hills above Hollywood, Steele becomes the prime suspect, particularly in the eyes of the police captain Lochner who is appalled at Steele's callous, even flippant reaction to the news of Mildred's murder: "Okay, arrest me for lack of emotion." As it turns out, one of the detectives on the case is Steele's old army buddy Nicolai. But even Nicolai has his doubts: "None of us could ever figure him out," he quips, referring to the army company Steele commanded. His doubts deepen when he invites Steele over for dinner and watches as the writer stages the murder as he imagines it. The camera intercuts Nicolai play-strangling his wife under Steele's direction with low angle close-ups of Steele becoming visually excited by the scene he is setting. Even Steele's long-term agent and friend, with whom he toys by hinting that he actually murdered Mildred, begins to believe Steele is guilty and immediately starts to make plans for his escape. The only person who seems solidly behind Steele is Laurel. After a series of double entendres and witty ripostes – pro forma for noir films – such as "We'll have dinner tonight, but not together," Laurel and Steele become lovers. Under her motherly care he begins to write again while cutting back on his drinking. She continues to defend her lover, even when called in again by Lochner who shows her Steele's extensive record of violent altercations.

Gradually, as the honeymoon period of their affair begins to dissipate, Laurel begins to doubt Steele as well. In fact, by this time even the audience may be sharing her doubts because Dixon's callousness and violent nature cannot help but colour the viewer's natural sympathy towards the star of the movie, particularly as it is Humphrey Bogart whose performances in other noir classics like *The Maltese Falcon* (1941) and *The Big Sleep* (1946) had always been tinged with violence and ambiguous motives. During a beach party with Laurel and the Nicolais, Steele finds out that Laurel had gone to the police station and not told him. He becomes enraged at this perceived act of betrayal and storms off. She follows him to his car and jumps in. Steele refuses to speak and instead terrifies her by driving around the mountain pass at breakneck speed and then crashing into another car. When the other driver becomes angered, Steele proceeds to beat him brutally and is about to smash his head in with a rock when Laurel's pleas stop him. He dismisses the incident by saying, "I've been in a hundred fights like that," and proceeds to put his

ABOVE
Still from 'Hangover Square' (1945)
Many noir protagonists are a little bit mad, and some are a lot mad. After hearing a discordant sound, composer George Harvey Bone (Laird Cregar) blacks out and commits murders at the request of his subconscious. Here he plays his final, bitter symphony.

LEFT
Still from 'Moonrise' (1948)
Danny Hawkins (Dane Clark) had been bullied by Jerry Sykes (Lloyd Bridges) for so many years that when he decides to fight back he delivers a killing blow. The state of his mind is unbalanced for the rest of the film.

OPPOSITE
Still from 'House by the River' (1950)
Not-so-successful novelist Stephen Byrne (Louis Hayward) accidently strangles his maid and tries to cover it up to protect his wife and good name. In a bizarre climax, as Stephen runs from apparitions he is wrapped in billowing curtains and strangled as he falls down the staircase.

119

ABOVE
Still from 'A Kiss Before Dying' (1956)
Upwardly mobile psycho killer Bud Corliss
(Robert Wagner) romances mining heiress
Dorothy Kingship (Joanne Woodward) and then
kills her when he realises her preganancy will get
her disinherited. Luckily there is a sister for him
to romance...

OPPOSITE
Still from 'The Lineup' (1958)
Dancer (Eli Wallach) is a career criminal who
does whatever is necessary, including killing The
Man (Vaughn Taylor) in his wheelchair. His
partner Julian sums up their attitude: "Women
have no place in society, they don't appreciate
the need for violence."

arm around Laurel in exactly the manner the authorities believe the killer used to strangle Mildred.

Laurel's faith in Steele is now broken. Even the dark romantic lines he speaks to her, taken from the script on which he is working – "I was born when you kissed me. I died when you left me. I lived a few weeks while you loved me" – cannot assuage her fear and distrust. She begins taking sleeping pills to avoid nightmares and seeks out friends like Nicolai's wife Sylvia to confide in. Soon she begins making plans for her escape, booking a flight for New York, even though she has agreed to marry Steele and travel to Las Vegas. She tells her plans to Mel, who advises that she make a clean break and be honest with Steele. She demurs: "I'm scared of him. I don't trust him."

The basis for this mistrust becomes fully realized in the final scene of the movie when Steele storms into her apartment and bullies her into going to Vegas with him: "Don't make me tell you again." When he discovers that she is planning to go to New York without him, he becomes crazed. He begins to strangle her, saying, "I'll never let you go." Only the sound of the phone ringing brings him to his senses. It is Lochner calling to say that Mildred's boyfriend has just confessed to the murder and apologizing for his harassment of the couple. As Steele walks disconsolately out the door and into the night, Laurel tells the captain forlornly, "It doesn't matter at all."

Still from 'Brute Force' (1947)
Watching prison movies like 'Riot in Cell Block 11' (1954), 'House of Numbers' (1957) and 'Brute Force' can be a lot like observing a pack of wild animals devour itself. Here guard informer Wilson (James O'Rear) is forced to his death under a punch press by Calypso (Sir Lancelot),

That statement is now not only true for Laurel but also for the audience. At this point it no longer matters whether Dixon Steele murdered Mildred that night. He has revealed himself to be capable of it. And that is all that matters for both his lover and the viewers in the audience. By the end of the film, whatever sympathy the viewer might have had for Steele has dissolved and what remains is the image of a violent, misogynistic man whose future is, like his mind, hopelessly clouded.

ABOVE
Still from 'Brute Force' (1947)
The inmates are tortured and exploited by the sadistic Captain Munsey, so prisoner Joe Collins organises a prison break. This is a living Hell from which there is no exit, for either the prisoners or the guards.

LEFT
On the set of 'Brute Force' (1947)
Director Jules Dassin (behind the camera) sets up a shot where Kid Coy (Jack Overman) saves Joe Collins (Burt Lancaster) during the prison break. The camera is mounted on the truck so that the action can be caught when the truck is moving at speed.

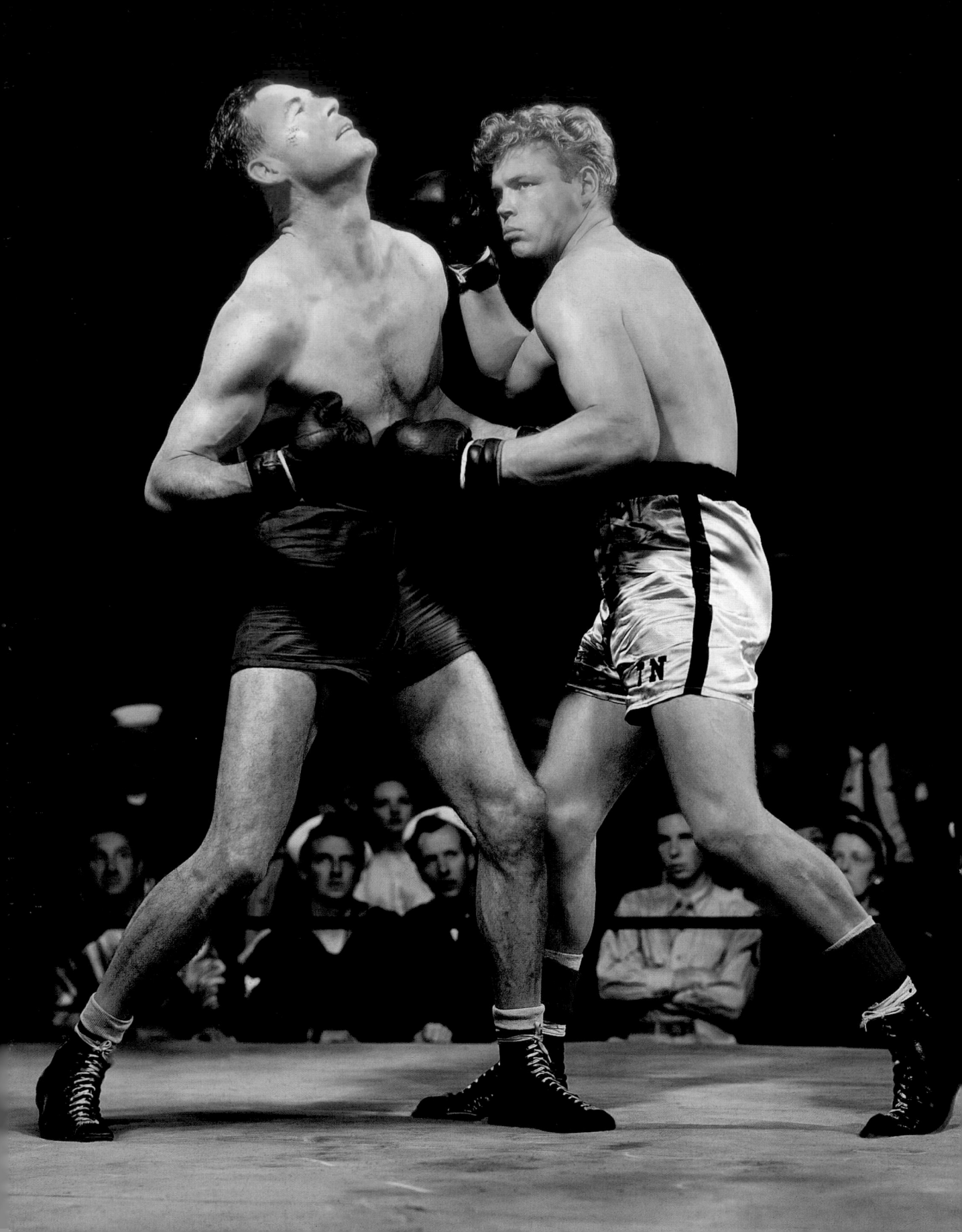

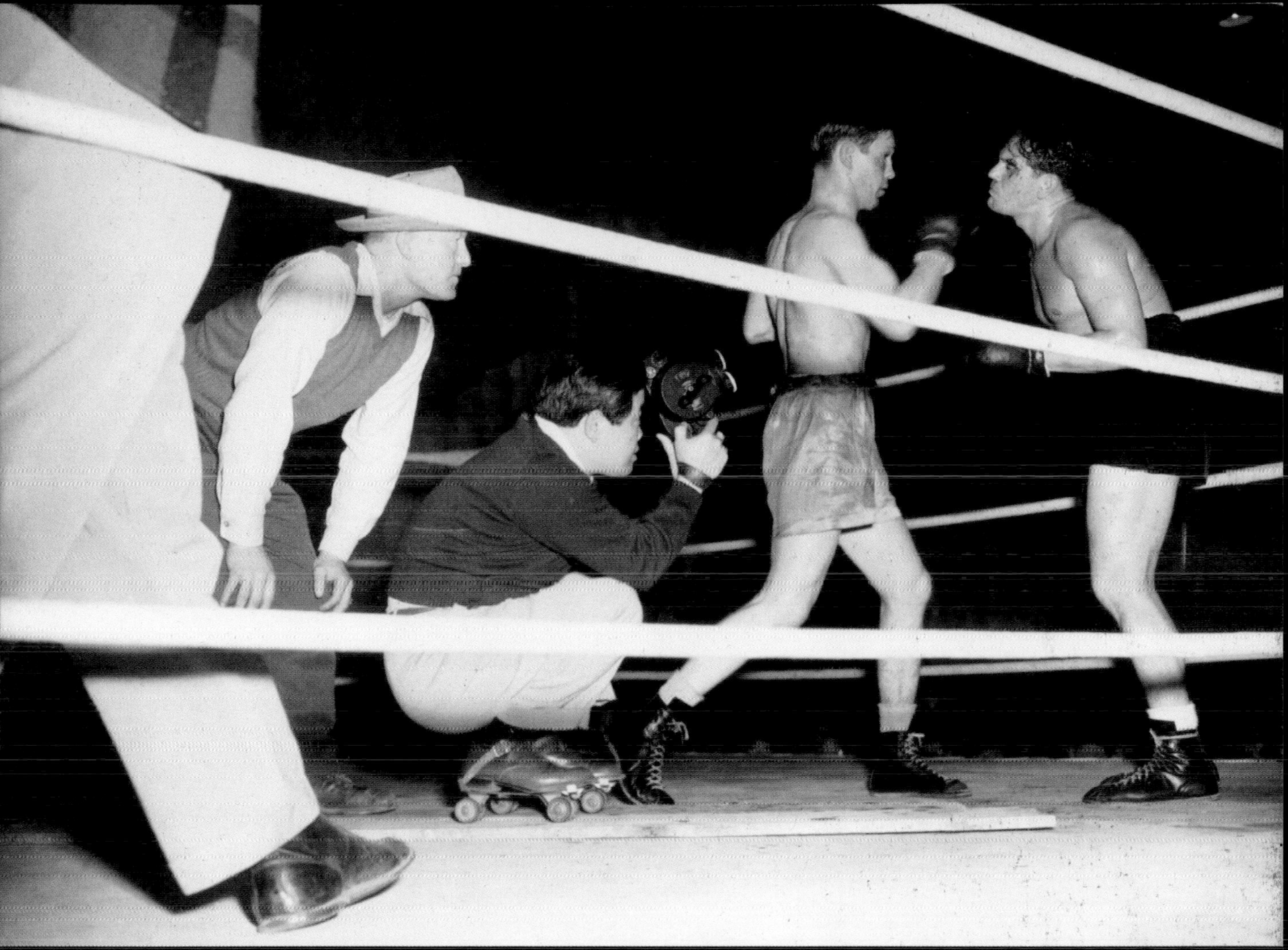

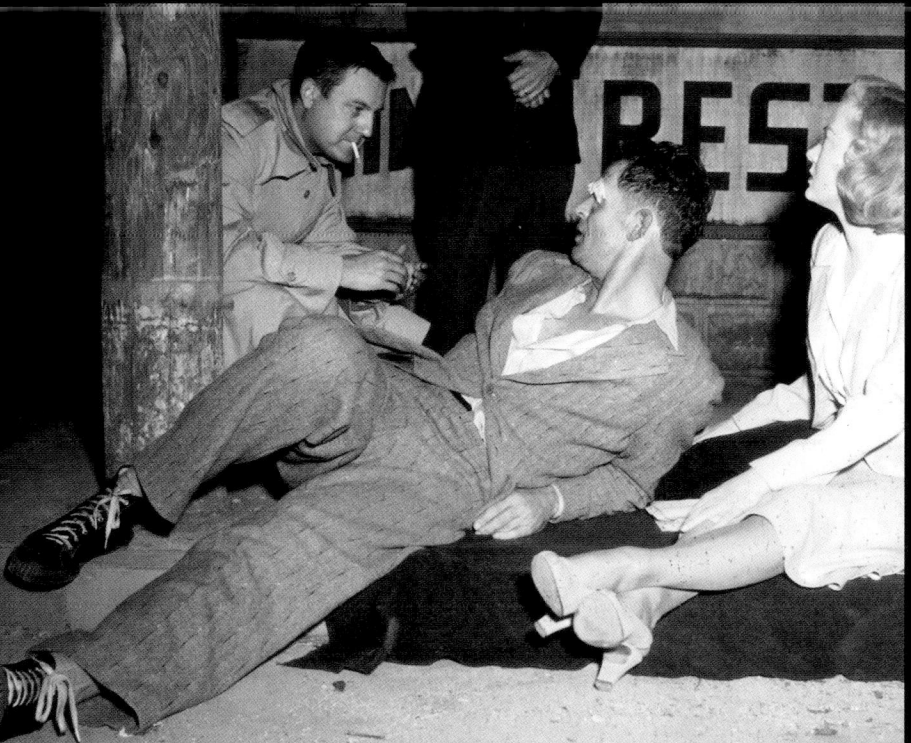

ABOVE

On the set of 'Body and Soul' (1947)
Men pummelling each other's flesh to a bloody pulp in a boxing ring is another male allegory for the hopelessness of existence in films like 'Champion' (1949), 'Body and Soul' and 'The Set-Up'. In this shot, master cameraman James Wong Howe uses roller skates to capture John Garfield as he takes some punishment.

LEFT
On the set of 'The Set-Up' (1949)
Robert Wise directs the final scene of the film, where a beaten Stoker Thompson (Robert Ryan) is cradled by his wife Julie (Audrey Totter). Stoker's body may be broken but his spirit isn't.

OPPOSITE
Still from 'The Set-Up' (1949)
Stoker takes a pounding in the early rounds, but his spirit and stamina give him the upper hand towards the end. It is only then that his manager tells him that he has to take a dive. When he doesn't, gangsters give him another beating.

ABOVE
Still from 'In a Lonely Place' (1950)
After a girl is strangled, screenwriter Dixon Steele (Humphrey Bogart) is accused of her murder. New neighbour Laurel Gray (Gloria Grahame) falls for Dixon but begins to suspect him when he almost beats a man to death. Here Dixon holds Laurel in the same way as the girl was strangled.

RIGHT
On the set of 'In a Lonely Place' (1950)
Director Nicholas Ray (right) watches Bogart and Grahame rehearse. Grahame was Ray's wife and the relationship in the film is said to have echoed their relationship.

OPPOSITE
Still from 'In a Lonely Place' (1950)
Dixon and Laurel are good for each other, but the tension generated by the murder investigation almost erupts into violence. When Laurel realises that Dixon is capable of murder, even though he is innocent of strangling the girl, their affair is over. Dixon is in a lonely place again.

Nicholas Ray

Nicholas Ray was born Raymond Nicholas Kienzle on 7 August 1911 in Galesville, Wisconsin. He attended the University of Chicago and then the University of Wisconsin, where he studied architecture under Frank Lloyd Wright. Concurrently he became interested in theatre, working as both an actor and a director. In 1932 he moved to New York where he worked with stage directors like Elia Kazan and John Houseman. During World War Two he wrote and directed radio propaganda for the Office of War Information. He returned to the theatre and then eventually worked as an assistant on films like Kazan's *A Tree Grows in Brooklyn* (1945). Houseman gave Ray his break as a director with *They Live by Night* (1948), although problems with Howard Hughes and RKO kept the film from being released until two years after shooting ~~*They*~~ *Live by Night* marked Ray's entry into the world of noir and was the beginning of a remarkable series of noir films in various genres including: *A Woman's Secret* (1949), *Knock on Any Door* (1949), *In a Lonely Place* (1950), *On*

Dangerous Ground (1952), *Johnny Guitar* (1954) and *Party Girl* (1958). His position in mainstream film history was secured with the James Dean vehicle *Rebel Without a Cause* (1955). Ray continued to produce off-beat films in various genres: Biblical epics such as *King of Kings* (1961), war films such as *Bitter Victory* (1957) and Westerns with *The True Story of Jesse James* (1957). Although he was lionized by the French critics at *Cahiers du cinéma* in the late 1950s and early 1960s, inspiring Jean-Luc Godard's memorably excessive comment, "Nicholas Ray is the cinema," he spent the last two decades of his life working erratically on personal projects like *You Can't Go Home Again* while appearing in films by admirers like Wim Wenders, with whom he co-directed the autobiographical documentary, *Lightning Over Water* (1980). Ray died of lung cancer in New York on 16 June 1979.

On the set of 'On Dangerous Ground' (1952)
Robert Ryan (right) plays brutal cop Jim Wilson ("Why do you punks make me do it?" he asks a suspect he is interrogating) whose natural sensitivity is revealed when he meets blind Mary Malden (played by Ida Lupino). Here director Nicholas Ray (centre) talks through a scene with the actors.

Women in Film Noir

While there are many female protagonists in film noir, most of them exist in tandem with a male figure. From *Double Indemnity* to *Gun Crazy*, no matter how dominating the woman may be, without a male figure of equal prominence there is no story, without a man to destroy there is no femme fatale. *Gilda* (1946) and *Nora Prentiss* (1947) are title characters and performers. In the patriarchal construction of film noir, it could be simplistically asserted that their talent can charm a man into self-destructive behaviour. But as those narratives demonstrate, Gilda and Nora are also victims of a society that both empowers and enslaves sexually potent woman.

Of the women who are principal characters in film noir, many are victims. In *Mildred Pierce* (1945), *The Damned Don't Cry* (1952) and *Sudden Fear* (1952) Joan Crawford portrayed women who endured mischance and betrayal but managed to survive. Both Norah Larkin in Fritz Lang's *The Blue Gardenia* (1953) and Wilma Tuttle in *The Accused* (1949) defend themselves by mortally wounding a sexual predator. While both are ultimately acquitted (Norah did not actually kill her assailant), both narratives turn dramatically on the women's sense of helplessness and both women are rescued by sympathetic men. In *The Blue Gardenia* Lang's fateful tracking shots encircle Norah to suggest that she cannot extricate herself without assistance, that only a male figure can save her from a whirlpool of doom. Other women, such as Paula Alquist in *Gaslight* (1944) and Leslie Calvin in *Dark Waters* (1946), are emotionally troubled and prey to psychological attack. Perhaps the most extreme example is Joseph H. Lewis' first film noir, *My Name is Julia Ross* (1945), in which the title figure is drugged, kidnapped and forced to assume a new identity. *No Man of Her Own* (1952), adapted from the Cornell Woolrich novel *I Married a Dead Man*, features a reverse plot in which a destitute woman is presented the opportunity to impersonate a wealthy young wife. But as directed by Mitchell Leisen, the emphasis is more on melodrama than fate.

Phantom Lady (1944), adapted from another Woolrich novel, is the first film noir with a true female protagonist. Like Kathleen, the secretary of private investigator Bradford Galt in *The Dark Corner* (1946), Carol 'Kansas' Richman is the only thing standing between her employer and the executioner. She launches her own investigation, going undercover to suffer advances from a lecherous musician, insults from a Brazilian diva and a narrow escape from becoming a victim herself. In *The Man I Love* (1946), which combines elements of noir and post-War readjustment in

'It is well worthwhile to ascertain how these ladies busy themselves all day... I cannot endure the woman who calculates, and commits a great crime in her sober senses.'

Juvenal, 'Satire VI'

ABOVE
Still from 'Laura' (1944)
In film noir the central male character often becomes obsessed with a woman, the femme fatale who is often the cause of his downfall or death. In 'Laura' police detective Mark McPherson (Dana Andrews) falls asleep in front of a portrait of the dead Laura Hunt (Gene Tierney) only to wake to find her in the room.

LEFT
Still from 'The Woman in the Window' (1945)
Mild-mannered Richard Wanley (Edward G. Robinson) becomes fascinated by a painting and then by the woman who posed for it. She leads him into dark places he would rather not visit.

OPPOSITE
Still from 'Gilda' (1946)
The vivacious and fun-loving Gilda (Rita Hayworth) is caught between husband Ballin Mundson and former lover Johnny Farrell.

133

the manner of *Best Years of Our Lives* and *Nobody Lives Forever* (both 1946), torch singer Petey Brown must balance job, love, family and finances, all whilst fending off the advances of her gangster boss. As Petey, Ida Lupino – who with *The Hitch-hiker* (1953) would become the only woman to direct a classic period noir – is as long-suffering as any Crawford character, as determined as Ella Raines' 'Kansas,' and as resourceful as most male figures in film noir.

Unlike Nora Prentiss or Gilda or Petey Brown, Lucia Harper in *The Reckless Moment* (1949) does not perform in nightclubs. She has no shady past. Rather she lives a comfortable life in upscale Balboa, California, with her husband, children, father-in-law, housekeeper and pets, until a large problem lands on her doorstep: her teenage daughter Bea has fallen for an older man named Darby, who is now dead.

The Reckless Moment is quite distinct in the noir cycle. The story is similar to *The Woman in the Window* (1945) and *Detour* in that an attempt to conceal a death results in blackmail. The crucial difference, of course, is that while its protagonist is as morally innocent as the male characters in those earlier films, the person enmeshed by circumstances in *The Reckless Moment* is a woman, a woman whose husband is away on business and who must deal with a catastrophe alone. (An interesting side-note: while these elements are in the novel by Elisabeth Sanxay Holding, that work was part of a series featuring a male hero, a police detective named Levy.)

As Lucia Harper, Joan Bennett, who happens to be the femme fatale of both *The Woman in the Window* and *Scarlet Street* (1945), is an ordinary woman, neither glamorous nor cunning. Somewhat like the women in *Mildred Pierce* or *The Accused*, the irony of her situation is not her innocence but that her middle-class values give her no pause before she decides to conceal a death by misadventure. Unlike Mildred Pierce, who protects her daughter Veda despite knowing that she has become a merciless and murderous schemer, Bea is an ostensibly normal if impressionable teenager and her involvement with Darby is a youthful error. Lucia's decision to try to shield her own family is parental instinct and perfectly normal. As compared to the ruthless ambition of Mildred Pierce, in which she sacrifices her marriage for the sake of business success and the social advancement of her daughter, or the sexual paranoia of Wilma Tuttle in *The Accused*, who lives an inculcated life as a prim academic, Lucia is entirely ordinary.

The visualization of director Max Ophüls stresses the commonplace aspects of Lucia's milieu. Unlike his earlier *Caught* (1949), in which the dark corners of her wealthy husband's mansion seemed to swallow the hapless Leonora Eames, the Harper house is well-lit, compact, tidy and filled with lived-in furnishings. Lucia's outfits, light-coloured suits and dresses, are fashionable but quite different from Alice Reed's elegant evening gown and dark shawl when she suddenly appears to Dr Wanley reflected as *The Woman in the Window*. With short hair, simple make-up and lighting that leaves her face free of shadows, Bennett is neither mysterious nor ominous.

As mundane as her surroundings may be, they fail to insulate Lucia from the encroachment of the noir underworld. Martin Donnelly, the would-be blackmailer whose infatuation with Lucia leads him to betray his cronies and assist her, may suggest that there are redeemable people in the noir underworld. In fact, Donnelly's fascination with Lucia is not realistic behaviour for a small-time crook. By casting against type and using suave British actor James Mason, Ophüls creates another anomaly. Donnelly becomes an introspective loner, as much out of place with his

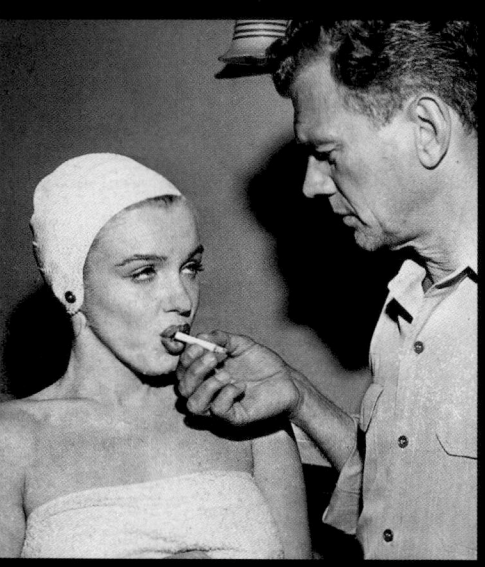

ABOVE
Still from 'Niagara' (1953)
Although there were restrictions as to what the film-makers could and could not show on the screen, the femmes fatales still managed to convey their sexual intentions. Here Rose Loomis (Marilyn Monroe) seduces her mentally unbalanced husband George (Joseph Cotten), whom she plans to kill.

OPPOSITE
Publicity still for 'The Big Heat' (1953)
Surely this is the most blatant use of a gun as phallic symbol. Debby Marsh (Gloria Grahame) is at the feet of former policeman Dave Bannion (Glenn Ford), who goes on his own personal rampage of revenge when his wife is killed by the syndicate chief.

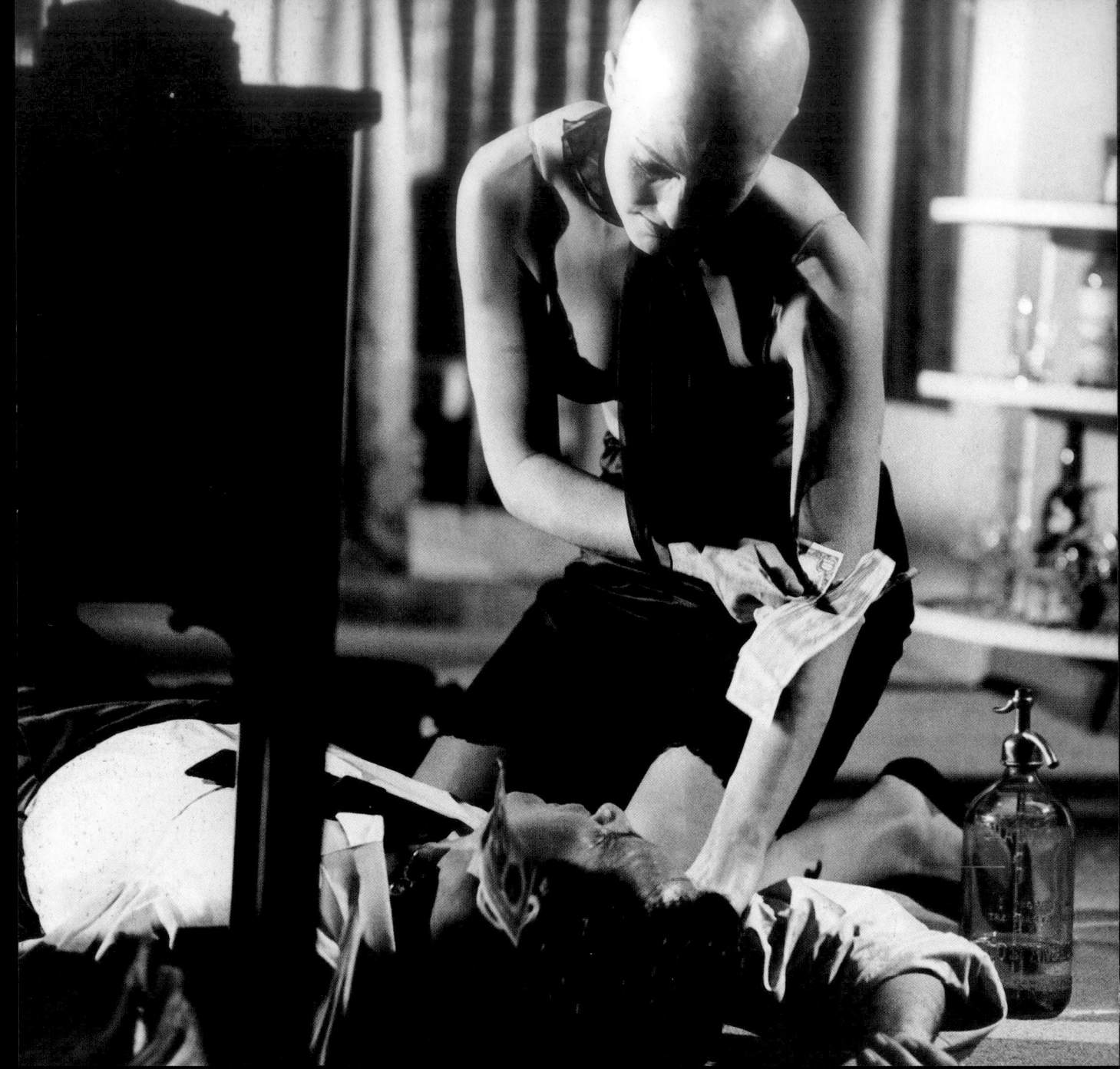

Still from 'The Naked Kiss' (1964)
In film noir, women have as much potential to be
killers as men. Here prostitute Kelly (Constance
Towers) beats her cheating pimp and takes the
money he owes her. Throughout the film her
moral outrage and willingness to do something
about it (she fills handicapped children full of
hope; she kills a child molester) puts her in the
same position as many male noir protagonists.

ABOVE
Still from 'Love Letters' (1945)
When Singleton (Jennifer Jones) finds out that
her boyfriend Roger Morland (Robert Sully, dead
body) isn't the sensitive man his letters led her to
believe, she cracks up and kills him. A year later,
Roger's friend and the real letter writer Allen
Quinton visits her in a prison hospital, where she
suffers from amnesia. He falls in love with her
and lives in fear that she will discover the truth
about him.

PAGES 138/139
Still from 'Leave Her to Heaven' (1945)
Ellen Berent (Gene Tierney) will stop at nothing
to make sure no one comes between her and her
husband Richard Harland. This includes letting
his crippled brother Danny (Darryl Hickman)
drown, and aborting her pregnancy by throwing
herself down the stairs.

ABOVE
Still from 'Caged' (1950)
Women go to prison too. Naïve Marie Allen
(Eleanor Parker) is jailed for being an accomplice
in an armed robbery, but prison turns her into a
hard-nosed con.

OPPOSITE TOP
Still from 'The File on Thelma Jordon' (1950)
Thelma Jordon (Barbara Stanwyck, right) is
accused of murdering her Aunt Vera.

OPPOSITE BOTTOM
On the set of 'I Want to Live!' (1958)
This film was based on the true story of Barbara
Graham, a woman of dubious moral standards
who was framed for murder and sentenced to
death by electric chair. Susan Hayward (centre)
won an Oscar for her performance in the lead
role and director Robert Wise (right) was also

accomplices in blackmail as he is with Lucia but perfectly suited to her needs. No matter how much Donnelly may aspire to Lucia's goodwill, it is a hopeless dream. Instinctively, unconsciously Lucia uses Donnelly. Aghast at the death and violence that have intruded into her placid life, Lucia fails to understand that the key to her salvation and that of her family is in her values, for that is what binds Donnelly to her and compels his sacrifice. On one level, Donnelly's death is useless. Since neither she nor Bea are really guilty of murder, he dies to save them from little more than embarrassment. On another level, the shock of his death makes clear to Lucia that the world will never be the same and that nothing should ever be taken for granted. Even as the momentarily disrupted facets of her life realign themselves, even as her world falls easily back into place, life will never be commonplace or ordinary again.

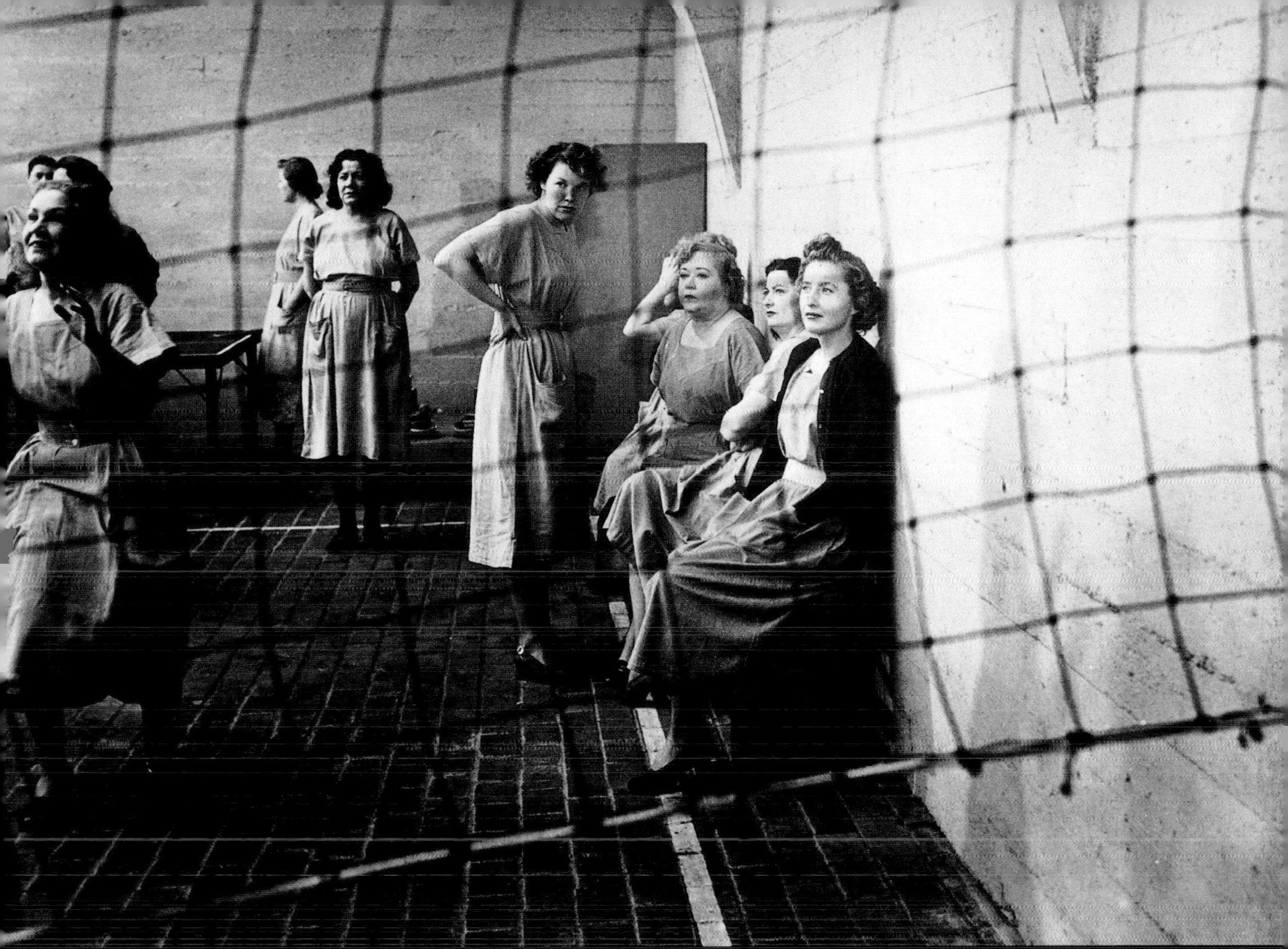

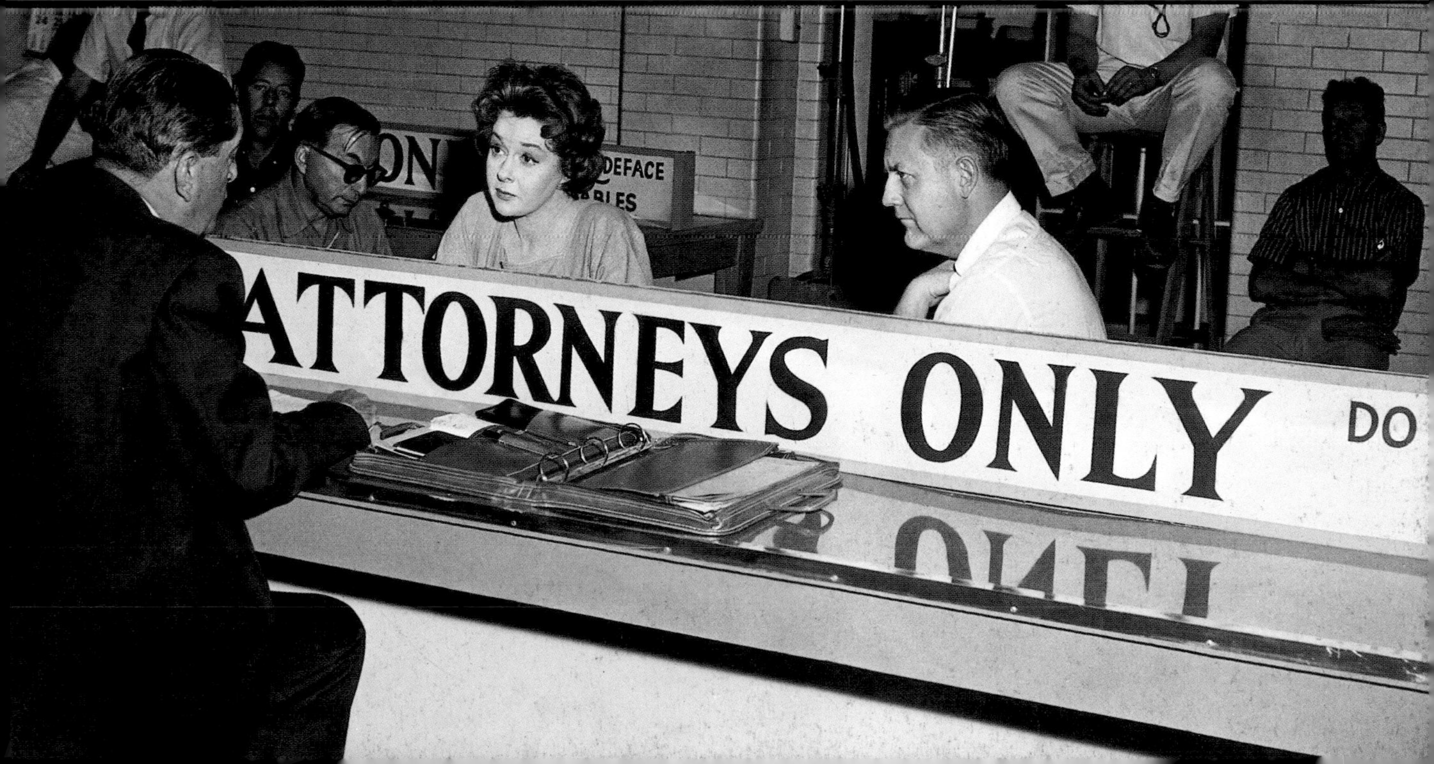
ATTORNEYS ONLY
DO
DEFACE

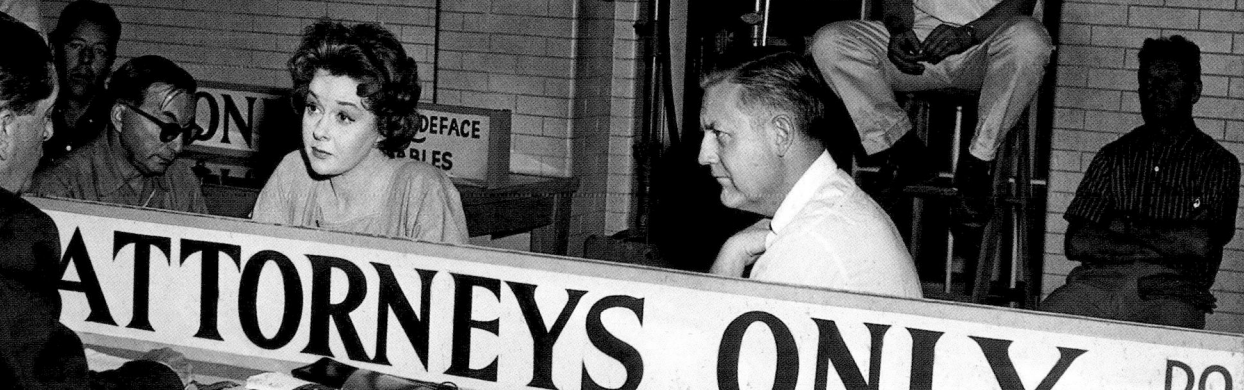

ABOVE
Still from 'The Reckless Moment' (1949)
Lucia Harper (Joan Bennett) finds the dead body of Ted Darby (Shepperd Strudwick) on the beach outside her home. Her daughter Bea was having an affair with this unscrupulous older man. Lucia disposes of the body, believing her daughter killed him.

RIGHT
Still from 'The Reckless Moment' (1949)
Martin Donnelly (James Mason, centre) arrives at the Harper home and blackmails Lucia with compromising letters written by Bea to the dead man. However, Martin becomes enamoured of the respectable family home and bends the rules at the risk of angering his violent boss Nagle.

Max Ophüls

Max Ophüls was born Max Oppenheimer in Saarbrücken, Germany on 6 May 1902. He declined to enter the family industry and decided to be a theatre critic and performer. He adopted his pseudonym and after a brief career as a stage actor Ophüls began directing plays in 1923, mounting productions of Shakespeare, Molière, Shaw and Schiller with companies in Stuttgart, Vienna, Frankfurt and Berlin. After 10 years of stage work, he began to work as an assistant film director for Anatole Litvak. With his extensive stage experience, Ophüls was soon directing 'talkies'; but in 1933 after a half dozen features, the Jewish Ophüls, like Siodmak and Wilder, left Nazi Germany for France. Between 1933 and 1940 Ophüls directed 10 feature-length films in France, Italy and Holland and even became a French citizen. In 1940 the German occupation forced him to flee again first to Switzerland and then to the United States. Ophüls had a difficult time adapting to Hollywood. In 1946, Preston Sturges hired him to direct *Vendetta* for Howard Hughes, only to fire him (the project had five directors, including Sturges, before it was finally released in 1950). He then made two period pictures at Universal with his colleague from

Still from 'The Reckless Moment' (1949)
After killing Nagle to prevent him hurting Lucia, Martin gives the letters back to Lucia. With his dying breath he confesses to the murders in front of the police, clearing Lucia and Bea of any involvement. Immediately after Martin's death, the Harper family returns to their middle-class existence as if nothing had happened.

"The masters of our profession... transcend both dramatic structure and dialogue, and create a new kind of tension which, I believe, has never existed before in any of the other forms of dramatic expression; the tension of pictorial atmosphere and of shifting images."

Max Ophüls [14]

Germany, Franz Planer, as cinematographer: *The Exile* (1947) and *Letter from an Unknown Woman* (1948). *Caught* and *The Reckless Moment* were Ophüls' last two American pictures, both released in 1949 and both classics of film noir. Ophüls returned to France after completing *The Reckless Moment* and made his last four films: *La Ronde* (1950), *Le Plaisir* (1951), *Madame de...* (1953) and *Lola Montès* (1955). If Ophüls' reputation as a stylist was ever in doubt, these final films dispelled that and carried him to the peak of critical acclaim in Europe. He died in Hamburg on 25 March 1957 but was buried at Père-Lachaise in Paris.

ABOVE
On the set of 'Caught' (1949)
James Mason, Barbara Bel Geddes and director Max Ophüls.

OPPOSITE
Still from 'Caught' (1949)
Leonora Eames (Barbara Bel Geddes) has been brainwashed by society into believing that money and power are to be desired and worshipped. When she marries millionaire Smith Ohlrig (Robert Ryan), he taunts and bullies her. Although she leaves for a time to work for Dr. Larry Quinada, and is happy with him, she always returns to Ohlrig and the false security of money.

The Maltese Falcon is the consensus starting point for the classic period, then the private eye is an icon of film noir from the first moment. Whatever he was called – gumshoe, peeper, private dick, op, snooper, or shamus – the prototype for the noir character came out of the hard-boiled school of crime stories, the penny-a-word pulp fiction that filled the pages of _Dime Detective_ and _Black Mask_ magazines from the early 1920s onwards.

The 'Continental Op,' a short, pudgy, long-in-the-tooth investigator was the usual protagonist in his mystery writing, but Dashiell Hammett, himself an alcoholic ex-private eye, is best remembered for creating Sam Spade. Hammett drew liberally from his own experiences (which were later novelized by Joe Gores and made into the 1982 movie _Hammett_ by Wim Wenders) for _The Maltese Falcon_. The version released in 1941 and considered by many to be the starting point of film noir's classic period was actually the third adaptation of Hammett's book by Warner Bros. and was previously adapted under that title in 1931 and as _Satan Met a Lady_ in 1936. Propitiously, as the kick-off for the noir cycle, the John Huston adaptation quickly became and has remained the definitive version; and Humphrey's Bogart's nuanced performance as Spade set the standard for all the noir PIs to follow.

In his essay 'The Simple Art of Murder,' Raymond Chandler, another graduate of the pulps, wrote what has become the definitive description (cited below) of the private eye in fiction. After a bizarre metamorphosis in which his character, Philip Marlowe, became the Falcon in 1942's _The Falcon Takes Over_ and then Mike Shayne in _Time to Kill_ the following year, Chandler's first four novels and his untarnished and unafraid hero became a staple of 1940s noir. RKO cast Dick Powell as Marlowe in _Murder My Sweet_ (1944). With the signature set design and low-key lighting of the studio which financed both _Citizen Kane_ and Val Lewton's series of atmospheric horror films, _Murder My Sweet_ is a stylistic tour-de-force set almost entirely at night or inside the uniformly under-lit interiors of musty offices, cheap bars, tract houses and Bel-Air mansions. The best-known sequence in the picture is a hallucinatory episode of exaggerated sights and sounds that is meant to express a drugged Marlowe's mental state.

Bogart moved from Spade to Marlowe in _The Big Sleep_ (1946), his second teaming with director Howard Hawks and co-star Lauren Bacall. Writers William Faulkner and the young Leigh Brackett – Hawks thought she was a man before their

'Down these mean streets a man must go who is not himself mean, who is neither tarnished nor afraid. The detective in this kind of story must be such a man. He is the hero; he is everything. He must be a complete man and a common man and yet an unusual man. He must be, to use a rather weathered phrase, a man of honor – by instinct, by inevitability, without thought of it, and certainly without saying it. He must be the best man in his world and a good enough man for any world.'

Raymond Chandler, 'The Simple Art of Murder'

ABOVE
Publicity still for 'The Maltese Falcon' (1941)
Sam Spade presents 'the black bird' to the
murderous creatures obsessed by it: effeminate
Joel Cairo (Peter Lorre), aloof bitch Brigid
O'Shaughnessy and cultured thug Kasper
Gutman (Sydney Greenstreet).

RIGHT
Still from 'The Maltese Falcon' (1931)
In the first film version of Dashiell Hammett's
novel, Private Operative Samuel Spade (Ricardo
Cortez) is much more of a ladies man, seemingly
bedding everything in a skirt (or out of it). Here
he and sexy secretary Effie Perrine (Una Merkel)
must decide what to do with 'the black bird'.

*"I hope you're not letting yourself be influenced
by the guns these pocket edition desperados are
waving around, because I've practiced taking guns
from these boys before so we'll have no trouble
there."*

Sam Spade (Humphrey Bogart) in *The Maltese Falcon* **(1941)**

Still from 'The Maltese Falcon' (1931)
When femme fatale Ruth Wonderly (Bebe
Daniels) stays overnight at Sam's apartment,
Sam takes the opportunity to ransack her hotel
room looking for money and clues. His desire for
money is practical, and reinforces the point that
he is a businessman, not a knight errant.

LEFT
Still from 'The Maltese Falcon' (1941)
Although Spade is emotionally involved with
Brigid, he lets her take the fall for the murder of
his partner Miles Archer (Jerome Cowan, left).
Spade tells her: "When one of your organisation
gets killed it's bad business to let the killer get
away with it."

PAGES 150/151
Publicity still for 'Murder, My Sweet' (1944)
Philip Marlowe (Dick Powell) is surprised by
Moose Malloy (Mike Mazurki), recently out of
prison and looking for his beloved Velma.

first meeting; Bogart called her 'Butch' and would let no one else touch his dialogue – recast Chandler's violent and convoluted plot, which left bodies piled up from Malibu to San Bernardino, into a backdrop for a sharp-tongued film noir courtship between a down-to-earth Marlowe and spoiled heiress Vivian Sternwood. In 1947 Robert Montgomery directed and portrayed Marlowe in *The Lady in the Lake*, although in this most idiosyncratic film noir the audience only got a good look at him when he stood in front of a mirror, because Montgomery adapted Chandler's first-person prose in the most literal way: the entire film was shot in subjective camera. Being locked into Marlowe's point of view created some unusual scenes, as when Marlowe is struck and doused with liquor which prompts the camera to crawl across a roadway, lurch into a phone booth and struggle to reach up and drop a dime to call for help.

The noir cycle may give the impression that many of its heroes were private investigators. In fact, aside from the pictures adapted from the novels of Chandler and Hammett there are very few. There are other amateur sleuths, of course, such as the journalists in *The Big Clock* or *Call Northside 777* (both 1948), and the insurance men in *The Killers* (1946) or *Pitfall* (1948). There are also amnesiacs seeking their own pasts, as in *Street of Chance* (1942) or *Somewhere in the Night* (1946), resourceful secretaries, as in *Phantom Lady*, and even paranoid children as in *Talk About a Stranger* (1952). However, most of the detectives in film noir are public servants, whether with a local police force or a federal agency.

There are few actual PIs outside the universe of Hammett or Chandler in 1940s film noir. Jeff Bailey in *Out of the Past* and Bradford Galt in *The Dark Corner* are among those few. It may have been nearly a decade later but it was only a short step in the noir underworld from Galt's dark corner to the shadowy locales of 1954 Los Angeles in Robert Aldrich's *Kiss Me Deadly* (1955). At the core of this film are speed and violence. This adaptation of Mickey Spillane's novel relocates Mike Hammer from New York to Los Angeles and situates him in a landscape of sombre streets and decaying houses even less inviting than those stalked by Spade and Marlowe. Like Hammer's sports cars, the movie swerves frenziedly through a series of disconnected and cataclysmic scenes. As it typifies the frenetic, post-Bomb L.A. of the 1950s with its malignant undercurrents, it also records the degenerative half-life of an unstable noir universe moving towards critical mass. When it reaches the fission point, the graphic threat of machine-gun bullets traced in the door of a house on Laurel Canyon in *The Big Sleep* is superseded to the nth degree as a beach cottage in Malibu becomes ground zero.

From the beginning, *Kiss Me Deadly* is a true sensory explosion. In the pre-credit sequence, a woman stumbles out of the pitched darkness, while her breathing fills the soundtrack with amplified, staccato gasps. Blurred metallic shapes flash by without stopping. She positions herself in the centre of the roadway, until oncoming headlights blind her with the harsh glare of their high beams. Brakes grab, tires scream across the asphalt and a Jaguar spins off the highway in a swirl of dust. A close shot reveals Hammer behind the wheel. Over the panting and the sound of a jazz piano on the car radio, the ignition grinds repeatedly when he tries to restart the engine. Finally, he snarls at the woman, "You almost wrecked my car! Well? Get in!"

From the opening dialogue between Hammer and Christina, *Kiss Me Deadly* establishes another sort of hero: one that is sneering, sarcastic and not really a hero at all. Hammer doesn't care who the woman is, that she seems to be naked under an overcoat or that she talks in riddles. She's just "a fugitive from the laughing house."

ABOVE
On the set of 'Murder, My Sweet' (1944)
Edward Dmytryk directs and Claire Trevor listens. Dmytryk was one of the Hollywood Ten jailed by the House Un-American Activities Committee for his Leftist views. After several months in jail he named people, and became part of an all-too-noir world.

OPPOSITE
Still from 'Murder, My Sweet' (1944)
Femme fatale Velma/Mrs Grayle (Claire Trevor) holds Marlowe's hands suggestively. An excellent actress, Trevor specialised in floozies and molls like Dallas in 'Stagecoach' (1939), Pat Cameron in 'Raw Deal' (1948) and Gaye Dawn in 'Key Largo' (1948).

"'Okay Marlowe,' I said to myself. 'You're a tough guy. You've been sapped twice, choked, beaten silly with a gun, shot in the arm until you're crazy as a couple of waltzing mice. Now let's see you do something really tough, like putting your pants on.'"

Philip Marlowe (Dick Powell) in *Murder, My Sweet* (1944)

ABOVE
Still from 'Murder, My Sweet' (1944)
Marlowe is blinded by a gun flash. He is also blind in other ways. The film is a series of sudden flashes of light, or depths of darkness.

LEFT
Still from 'Murder, My Sweet' (1944)
The film is presented in flashback as Marlowe recounts to the police the events that led to his blindness. This gives a reason for his narration, and also allows him to comment on the parade of grotesques he meets during his seach for Velma.

155

Yet within a few seconds, she has Hammer pegged. "You're angry with me aren't you?" she asks rhetorically. "Sorry I nearly wrecked your pretty little car. I was just thinking how much you can tell about a person from such simple things. Your car, for instance." "Now what kind of message does it send you?" Hammer asks out of the side of his mouth. It's an easy call for her. "You have only one real lasting love: You. You're the kind of person who never gives in a relationship, who only takes." Then her reverie turns sardonic, even mockingly dreamy: "Ah, woman, the incomplete sex. And what does she need to complete her? One man, wonderful man!"

What kind of hero is this Mike Hammer? *Kiss Me Deadly*'s opening dialogue types him quickly. Christina's accusation of narcissism merely confirms what the icons suggest about 'how much you can tell about the person from such simple things': the sports car, the trench coat, the curled lip, the jazz on the radio. Aldrich and screenwriter A.I. Bezzerides merely use Christina to explain and reinforce what the images have already suggested, that this is not a modest or admirable man. The dialogue also reveals that Hammer knows exactly who he is and the image he presents: 'What kind of message does it send you?' It sends the one Hammer wants to send, a message that even a fugitive from the "laughing house" can read loud and clear.

ABOVE
Still from 'The Big Sleep' (1946)
Philip Marlowe (Humphrey Bogart) has learned that everybody he trusts ends up dead. After several verbal duels with the feisty Vivian Sternwood (Lauren Bacall) they decide to trust each other and she releases him. This scene was one of many that benefitted Bacall when it was refilmed. Between the end of filming in January 1945 and its release in August 1946, director Howard Hawks reshot about 15 minutes of the film to tighten it up and to spice up the relationship between Marlowe and Vivian.

OPPOSITE
Still from 'The Big Sleep' (1946)
Carmen Sternwood (Martha Vickers) is as high as a kite while Arthur Gwynne Geiger (Theodore Von Eltz) lies dead at her feet. Marlowe has been hired by General Sternwood to deal with Geiger, who had compromising pictures of Carmen, but the case turns out to be far more complicated than that.

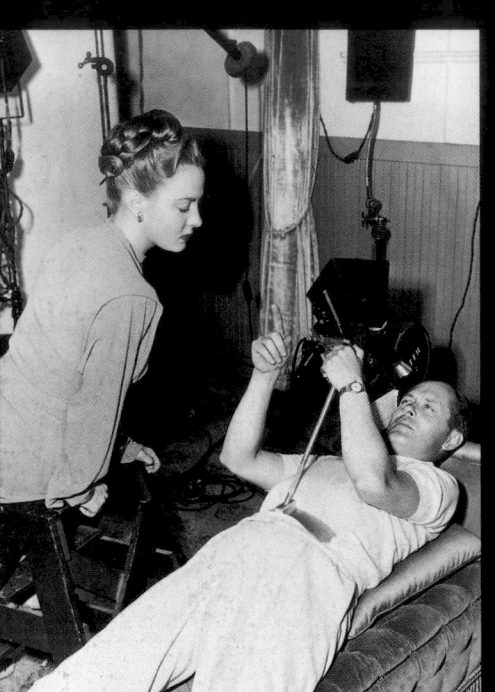

On the set of 'The Lady in the Lake' (1947)
Actor/Director Robert Montgomery translated the first person narration of Raymond Chandler's Philip Marlowe novels into film technique by only filming from Philip Marlowe's point of view. As you can see, a special attachment to the camera made sure that the film was always at his eyeline. Audrey Totter waits to get in the frame.

The dark highway of the opening is a kind of narrative limbo: the elements of the plot have not yet been revealed, let alone focused. The countryside and the rural gas station are all unidentified settings. They are open, murky and, even within the fringes of the station's neon lights, menacing. Certainly by the time of *Kiss Me Deadly*'s release in 1955, contemporary viewers had formed expectations about character and plot from the conventions of film noir. Mickey Spillane's original novel also set a tone:

> 'All I saw was the dame standing there in the glare of the headlights waving her arms like a huge puppet and the curse I spit out filled the car and my own ears. I wrenched the car over, felt the rear end start to slide, brought it out with a splash of power and almost ran up the side of the cliff as the car fishtailed. The brakes bit in, gouging a furrow in the shoulder, then jumped to the pavement and held. Somehow I had managed a sweeping curve around the babe.'

Spillane's considerable popularity as a novelist derived from his obvious objectification of women which coupled neatly with his lurid sadomasochism and his rabid 'red-baiting' in the shadow of McCarthy. While Aldrich and Bezzerides take a few events and little else from Spillane, his recurring protagonist, Hammer, provides the predetermined viewpoint, brought out mostly by his overwrought wisecracks and overheated narration like a poor man's Marlowe. Aldrich and Bezzerides abandon most of this also or rather, in Aldrich's preferred method, they 'stand it on its head.' Of the opening dialogue only one line is from the novel; but much more is changed than just the words. Most of the movie's elaborate plot, in which Hammer uses clues ranging from a locker key to a poem by Christina Rossetti to find a mysterious container his girl friend Velda dubs the "great what's it," is the invention of the film-makers.

In terms of attitude, on film Spillane's Hammer is even more of a grinning predator. He is the antithesis of Chandler's urban knight, with survival instincts sharper even than Sam Spade's. Even Spillane's character has some glimmer of sympathy for a "damn-fool crazy Viking dame with holes in her head" and follows the trail of those who tried to kill him out of simple-minded outrage at their misdeeds: "I wouldn't need to look at their faces to know I was killing the right ones. The bastards, the dirty, lousy bastards!" The film Hammer is incorporated into a more sophisticated system that combines the undertone of film noir with the moral determinism of Aldrich and Bezzerides. While Hammer wants to know "what's in it for me?" all around him crime breeds counter-crime and thieves and murderers fashion the implements of their own destruction. For Spillane, Hammer's very name revealed all: a hard, heavy, unrelenting object pounding away mindlessly at social outcasts like two-penny nails. The film-makers refine this archetype slightly: Hammer does think, mostly about how to turn a buck. Christina is arguably the most conventionally sensitive of the picture's characters, so it is not without irony that she is the loony, the one institutionalized by society, yet quickest to penetrate Hammer's tough-guy pose. As Ralph Meeker's interpretation propels Hammer beyond the smugness and self-satisfaction of the novel into a blacker, more sardonic disdain for the world in general, the character becomes a cipher for all the unsavoury denizens of the noir underworld.

Hammer first asks, "What's in it for me?" when he speaks to his friend, detective Pat Murphy. That utterance completes the character composite: Hammer may not

be quite as selfless as Galahad as he begins a quest for 'something big,' for the private eye's grail, but Hammer is a quester. He is not an outsider in the world of film noir. Hammer is at home there. The dark streets and ramshackle buildings are a questing ground conspicuously detached from the commonplace world. Deception is the key to this world. Deception not detection is Hammer's trade. His livelihood depends on the divorce frame-up and the generally shady deal. Failure to deceive is what costs Christina and other victims their lives.

This deception and uncertainty, as in most noir films, laid the groundwork for *Kiss Me Deadly*'s melodramatic tension. The plotline has all the stability of one of Nick the mechanic's expressions: "Va-va-voom. Pretty pow!" For those on a quest in the noir underworld, instability is the overriding factor and disjunction is the rule, which the sensational elements in *Kiss Me Deadly* follow: the craning down and the hiss of the hydraulic jack as a screaming Nick is crushed under the weight of a car; the pillar of fire that consumes Lily Carver; the morgue attendant's scream as Hammer tortures him for information. These quasi-random events have no organizing principles. They transcend context to deliver a shock that is purely sensory.

'A savage lyricism hurls us into a decomposing world ruled by perversity and brutality,' wrote Raymond Borde and Etienne Chaumeton about *Kiss Me Deadly* in

ABOVE
Still from 'The Lady in the Lake' (1947)
Philip Marlowe (Robert Montgomery) examines his wounds in front of mercenary editor Adrienne Fromsett (Audrey Totter). The story takes a back seat to the film's enjoyable technique. As in real life, although Marlowe may be talking to one person, he can be looking at another.

PAGE 160
Still from 'Talk About a Stranger' (1952)
Not all investigators are licensed. In 'The Window' , 'Fallen Idol' and 'Talk About a Stranger', the protagonists are children. Here Bud Fontaine, Jr. (Billy Gray) meets Matlock (Kurt Kasznar), who he believes poisoned his dog. The cinematography is by the fabulous John Alton.

PAGE 161
On the set of 'Eyes in the Night' (1942)
Director Fred Zinnemann (on camera, top left) has good reason to keep it dark; his main character is a blind man investigating a murder.

ABOVE
Still from 'Kiss Me Deadly' (1955)
After the death of Christina, Mike Hammer tracks down her roommate Lily Carver (Gaby Rodgers), who is scared. She says it's like getting on a merry-go-round and then it goes so fast you can't get off again.

RIGHT
Still from 'Kiss Me Deadly' (1955)
Velda (Maxine Cooper) gives Mike Hammer (Ralph Meeker) the lowdown as she practices her ballet moves. Hammer doesn't detect anything. He lets everybody else do the brain work.

"You're one of those self-indulgent males who thinks about nothing but his clothes, his car, himself."

**Christina (Cloris Leachman) to Mike Hammer in *Kiss Me Deadly*
(1955)**

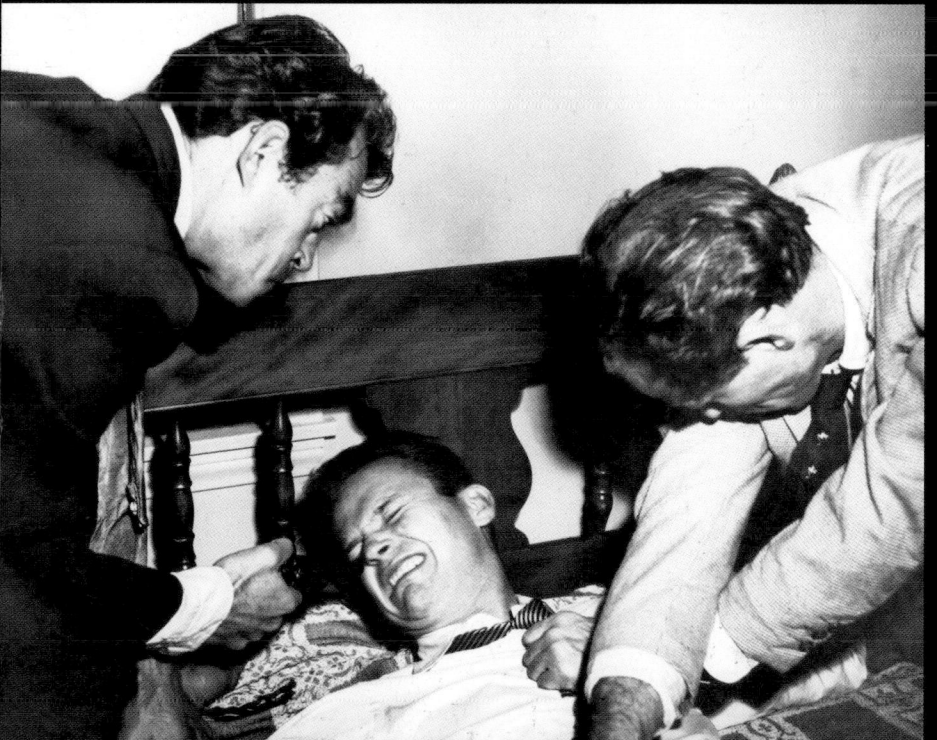

Still from 'Kiss Me Deadly' (1955)
Lily and Hammer enjoy a ride, but it is Hammer who is being taken for a ride. He is being deceived by Lily.

Still from 'Kiss Me Deadly' (1955)
The film is suffused with sudden violence. People are beaten up, cut, tortured and killed at a rapid pace throughout the film. One shock follows another. Here Hammer gets his make-up smudged courtesy of Charlie Max (Jack Elam) and Sugar (Jack Lambert).

"He gave me the Mickey Spillane book and I said, 'This is lousy. Let me see what I can do.'... I was having fun with it. I want to make every scene, every character interesting. A girl comes up to Ralph Meeker, so I make her a nympho. I'm a big car nut, so I put in all that stuff with the cars and the mechanic. I was an engineer so I gave the detective the first phone answering machine in that picture. I was having fun."

Screenwriter A.I. Bezzerides [15]

their pioneering study *Panorama du film noir américain*, after which 'Aldrich brings to bear the most radical of solutions: nuclear apocalypse.' Running parallel to Hammer's search is the meaning of the cryptic pentameters from the Rossetti poem: 'But when the darkness and corruption leave/A vestige of the thoughts that once we had.' Myth becomes a surface value entirely in the case of the 'great what's it' and nothing can prevent that Pandora's Box from opening. In the final analysis, the 'great what's it' contains pure phlogiston, the mythical element that is entirely combustible. The quest for it becomes the quest for the cleansing, combustible element, for the spark of the purifying fire that reduces the nether world of *Kiss Me Deadly* to radioactive ash, that according to Borde and Chaumeton gives film noir itself 'a fascinating and shadowy conclusion... the despairing opposite of the film which, fourteen years earlier opened the noir cycle, *The Maltese Falcon*.' As a coda for film noir, *Kiss Me Deadly* is an assonant vision of those powerful, malevolent forces lurking below the surface and then exploding in a mushroom cloud over Malibu.

Robert Aldrich

*"The original book, Kiss Me Deadly, had
nothing. We just took the title and threw the book
away. The scriptwriter, A.I. Bezzerides, did a
marvelous job. That devilish box, for example,
was mostly his idea. We worked a long time to
get the sound of it, the ticking and hissing. We
finally used the sound of an airplane exhaust
overdubbed with the sound made by human
vocal chords when someone breathes out noisily,
so that is became a subdued 'jet roar' you hear
every time the box opens."*

Producer/Director Robert Aldrich [16]

Robert Aldrich was born on 9 August 1918 in Cranston, Rhode Island. After prep
school, as befitted the son of a wealthy New England family, Aldrich played football
and studied economics at the University of Virginia but dropped out before
graduating. As the grandson of a United States senator and cousin to the
Rockefellers, Aldrich used his connections to secure a production clerk job at RKO
in 1941. With a football injury keeping him out of the wartime draft, Aldrich quickly
rose through the ranks as second and first assistant director then production
manager, working for such prominent directors as Jean Renoir, Lewis Milestone,
Joseph Losey, Robert Rossen, Abraham Polonsky and Charlie Chaplin. He learned
about movie-making on noir films such as *The Strange Love of Martha Ivers* (1946),
Body and Soul (1947), *Caught* (1949), *Force of Evil* (1948), *The Prowler* (1951) and *M*
(1951). Aldrich moved up to director in television, where he directed TV noir
starring Dick Powell for *Four Star Theater* and *China Smith* starring Dan Duryea. His
second feature and first film noir was an informal spin-off of the latter series, *World
for Ransom* (1954). Shortly thereafter Aldrich formed the first of many production
companies and produced many of his own features including *Kiss Me Deadly*. Over
the course of 30 features, he worked in almost every genre, his other noir films

being *The Big Knife* (1955) and *The Garment Jungle* (1957). His neo-noirs *The Grissom Gang* (1971) and *Hustle* (1975) were not fiscal successes, but *The Dirty Dozen* (1967) and *The Longest Yard* (1974) were. Aldrich's efforts to maintain his own production company and creative independence succumbed to changing tastes and practices in Hollywood by the 1980s. After several disappointing final films, Aldrich took himself off dialysis and died in Los Angeles on 5 December 1983.

Still from 'Whatever Happened to Baby Jane?' (1962)
Crippled Blanche Hudson (Joan Crawford) is kept imprisoned by her sister Jane (Bette Davis in Robert Aldrich's surprise hit.

The Darkness and Corruption

Noir always had a conscience. That is probably why so many leftists and blacklistees like Jules Dassin (*The Naked City*), Joseph Losey (*The Prowler*), Edward Dmytryk (*Cornered*), Albert Maltz (*The Naked City*), Adrian Scott (*Crossfire*) and Dalton Trumbo (*Gun Crazy*) found it such a salutary medium in which to work. Noir film-makers saw society from the perspective of down below, from the point of view of the loser, the criminal, the luckless individual or the proletarian everyman, so it was natural that noir would involve a significant amount of social critique. Blacklistee Abraham Polonsky's *Force of Evil* (1948) tells the story of an amoral gambling syndicate lawyer (John Garfield) who finds redemption in his deep love for a brother who is first harassed and then killed by the mob. Similarly, in *Rogue Cop* (1954), 'cop-on-the-take' Kelvaney (Robert Taylor) only sheds his corrupt mantle after his brother is murdered by the mob. He finds his own form of penance and redemption in a hail of bullets in the final shootout. In *I Wake Up Screaming* (1942) and its remake *Vicki* (1953), a dour and alienated police detective uses his official power to pursue his sexual/romantic obsession with a model and then after her death to persecute her fiancé. Dave Bannion in *The Big Heat* has already been cited: after the murder of his wife, an upstanding cop turns to questionable methods with fatal results. In *The Big Combo* (1955), directed by *Gun Crazy*'s Joseph H. Lewis, police detective Leonard Diamond (Cornel Wilde) permits a sexual obsession with the abused and masochistic socialite Susan Lowell (Jean Wallace) to alter his formerly legal modus operandi. He becomes intent on destroying the illegal operation of her mobster lover and his rival, Mr. Brown (Richard Conte), by any means necessary. In *Shockproof* (1949), written by noir scenarist-director Samuel Fuller (*Pickup on South Street*, 1953, *The Crimson Kimono*, 1959), a parole officer (also portrayed by Cornel Wilde) falls in love with a sultry parolee (Patricia Knight) and proceeds to dismantle his career, abandoning his strict sense of ethics in order to help her escape the law.

Touch of Evil was directed by Orson Welles, whose protean *Citizen Kane* is an acknowledged seminal influence on noir for its visual invention and its corrosive characterizations and even its stylized dialogue. *Touch of Evil* is a tale of corruption of Shakespearean dimensions. The film is set in a sleazy border town (the actual location used was Venice, California), where drug dealing, the sex trade, gambling and generally illicit behaviour runs rampant. "All border towns bring out the worst of a country," Vargas (Charlton Heston) tells his American wife (Janet Leigh). The

'Power tends to corrupt, and absolute power corrupts absolutely. Great men are almost always bad men.'

Lord Acton

famous opening sequence, a long craning and panning shot that lasts for over three minutes and ends with a car exploding, deftly establishes the milieu and its underlying violence. The shot opens on a homemade bomb being planted in the trunk of a car owned by a married American businessman named Linnekar, who is returning from a night of carousing with a stripper. The camera follows the car through the Mexican side of the border town, giving the viewer a glimpse into the dark streets and the rowdy denizens. It also picks up the two main protagonists of the movie, an incorruptible Mexican policeman named Vargas and his new wife Susan, who are on their honeymoon. As Vargas and Susan kiss, the camera finally cuts and reveals the car torn apart and consumed by flames.

This event is the trigger for a plot filled with by-now prototypical noir twists and turns, as Vargas joins his colleague north of the border, Detective Hank Quinlan, to find the perpetrator. Quinlan, as played by Welles himself, epitomizes corruption. He is a racist. When he finds out Vargas is on the case he says disdainfully, "They invited some sort of Mexican," and later he tells his detective partner, Pete Menzies, pointing to the U.S. side of the border, "Let's go back to civilization." He is also proud of the fact that he depends upon his 'intuition' rather than 'simple facts' and so is willing to employ questionable methods, such as beating Mexican suspect Sanchez, who is having an affair with the murdered man's daughter. Ultimately Quinlan plants dynamite in their 'love nest' bathroom to incriminate Sanchez. But what is most striking is Quinlan's physical appearance. Most often shot in low angle, Quinlan looks much like a bloated corpse long before he *is* one at the end of the movie. Munching on chocolate bars and limping with a cane, he seems to be infected and decaying physically as well as spiritually. As is later revealed by Menzies, Quinlan is also an alcoholic who fell apart after the strangulation murder of his wife, the only case he was not able to solve.

But the corruption in this film is not confined to Quinlan and his lackeys, which include district attorney Adair as well as the police chief. Welles intercuts the story of the investigation of the bombing with a parallel and sometimes overlapping tale of inbred crime, centring around the town boss, Uncle Joe Grandi. Akim Tamiroff, a frequent character actor for Welles, renders Grandi as quasi-comic figure with his Edward G. Robinson posturing and his misadjusted 'rug.' Grandi is also a crafty opportunist, who has decided to menace Vargas' wife in order to prevent him from testifying against his brother in Mexico City. His threats are met with defiance and disgust by Susan who calls him a "silly little pig." Grandi turns to more drastic measures while she is staying in a deserted motel in the desert, waiting for her husband to finish his investigation. In a suspenseful and terrifying scene, a group of thugs, including a lesbian couple, hired by Grandi surround the motel, blast music into her room for hours while she is trying to sleep. Eventually they cut off the lights before they attack and drug her. She is then dumped into a hotel in the border town.

The dual story threads begin to interweave neatly as Quinlan is accused by Vargas of planting evidence not only in this case but in former cases, which forces him to make overtures to Grandi, who tells Quinlan: "In this thing we are partners." To destroy Vargas' reputation, Quinlan, now 'off the wagon' and continuously drunk, meets Grandi in Susan's room. He strangles the hapless Grandi to implicate Vargas and Susan in murder; but Quinlan, whose mind is clouded by alcohol, makes a fatal error. He leaves his cane in the room.

Although still devoted to Quinlan, Menzies finds the cane and decides that he can no longer accept the misdeeds of his friend and mentor. He gives it to Vargas

The Committee for the First Amendment
Humphrey Bogart, Lauren Bacall, Danny Kaye, Paul Henreid, Richard Conte, Sterling Hayden, Gene Kelly, John Huston and others went to Washington to support the 'Unfriendly Nineteen' at the House Un-Amercan Activities Committee. The 'Hollywood Ten' refused to answer whether or not they were Communists and were jailed for contempt of court. Two years later the belligerant committee chairman J. Parnell Thomas was jailed for taking bribes.

Los Angeles, California Court (9 February 1949)
Robert Mitchum doesn't look too impressed when Superior Judge Clement D. Nye sentences him and actress Lila Leeds (left) to 60 days in jail for conspiracy to possess marijuana cigarettes. Mitchum was assigned 'The Big Steal' whilst in jail, so Don Siegel filmed the chase sequences without him, then later returned to the Mexican locations (in the heart of the marijuana-growing district) to do close-ups with Mitchum.

ABOVE
Still from 'Force of Evil' (1948)
Numbers man Leo Morse (Thomas Gomez,
centre) is betrayed by his bookkeeper Freddy
Bauer (Howland Chamberlain). Leo ("You're
dying while you're breathing") is kidnapped by a
rival gang whilst Freddy is unceremoniously
gunned down.

RIGHT
Still from 'Force of Evil' (1948)
Crooked lawyer Joe Morse (John Garfield), works
from a high office in Wall Street, but he has to go
down, down, down to the bottom of the world to
find the body of his brother Leo. Joe: "If a man's
life can be lived so long and come out this way,
like rubbish, then something was horrible, and
had to be ended one way or another, and I
decided to help."

Still from 'Rogue Cop' (1954)
Cop Christopher Kelvaney (Robert Taylor) is well dressed because he takes pay-offs from local criminals. When his brother becomes a cop and will not take the money and keep his mouth shut, Christopher is caught between his desires and his familial duties.

RIGHT
Still from 'I Wake Up Screaming' (1941)
Ed Cornell (Laird Cregar, left) is happy to see promoter Frankie Christopher (Victor Mature) go to the electric chair for the murder of his client actress Vicky Lynn based on circumstantial evidence. In truth Ed knows who the real killer is but is jealous of Frankie.

"*Experience has taught me never to trust a policeman. Just when you think one's all right, he turns legit.*"

Doc Riedenschneider (Sam Jaffe) in *The Asphalt Jungle* **(1950)**

Still from 'The Prowler' (1951)
Joseph Losey's film is about cop Webb Garwood (Van Heflin) who kills William Gilvray (Emerson Tracy) so that he can be with Susan Gilvray (Evelyn Keyes) and use the insurance money to set himself up in the motel business. This is a dark tale of the American Dream of success and status.

LEFT
On the set of 'The Third Man' (1949)
During a tea break, director Carol Reed (right) and actor Orson Welles (centre) discuss the famous scene in the ferris wheel where Harry Lime (Welles), looking down, compares people to insects and asks would you really care if one of those specks disappeared forever. Joseph Cotten (left) seems to be in a world of his own.

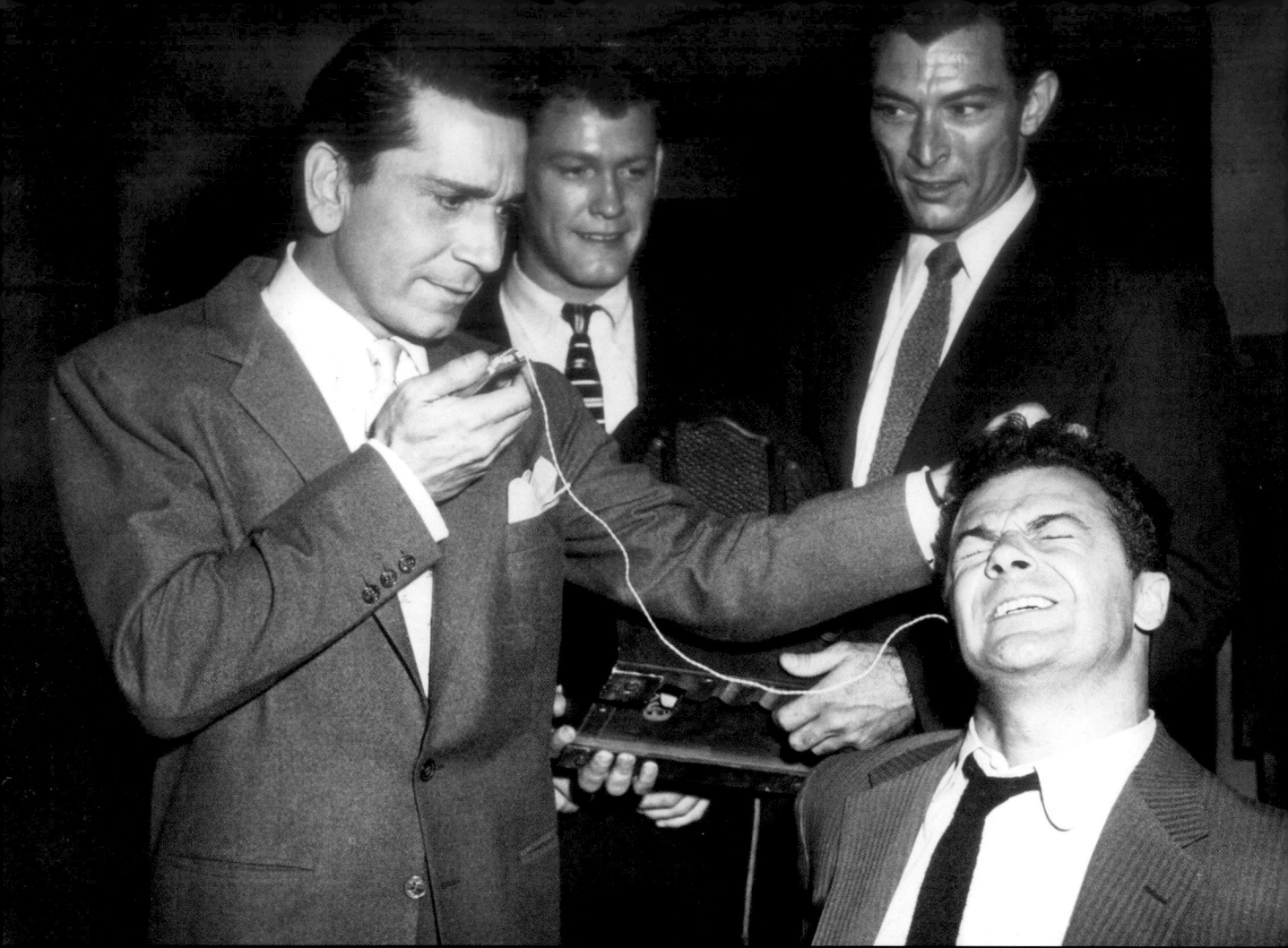

Still from 'The Big Combo' (1955)
Mr Brown (Richard Conte, left) tortures Detective Leonard Diamond (Cornel Wilde, right) using a hearing aid set on full volume. Diamond is harassing Mr Brown's organisation because he is obsessed with having Mr Brown's girlfriend Susan Lowell. Hitmen Mingo (Earl Holliman) and Fante (Lee Van Cleef) stand ready in the background.

but is distraught in the realization that this cannot be the first time that Quinlan has gone too far. Reluctantly, he agrees to wear a wire in order to record Quinlan's own incriminating words: "How do you think I feel about this? Hank is the best friend I ever had."

The final scene near the fetid canals and oil derricks of the town is a visual tour-de-force. The fluid camera follows Pete as he leads Quinlan along the canals while Vargas follows closely, hiding under bridges and behind derricks to stay within the limited range of the transmitter with the recording device. Quinlan is suspicious but drunk enough to confess that he did plant the dynamite in Sanchez's bathroom. Ultimately Quinlan's vaunted instincts kick in, as he senses Vargas' presence. He shoots Pete, whom he now realizes has betrayed him. The blood from his friend drips onto his hand. Using an extra wide-angle lens which distorts the scene, Quinlan wades out into the sewage-filled water and tries to wash the blood from his hands, evoking Lady Macbeth's famous scene in Shakespeare's play. Spotting Vargas, he turns to fire at him but is shot instead by a dying Menzies. Quinlan falls into the floating waste, which so clearly symbolizes the man's own corruption, as his bloated figure begins to drift out from the shore. Schwartz, a prosecutor who has helped Vargas, shows up with Susan and the surprising news that Sanchez has confessed and that, as Quinlan had insisted, the boy was guilty. This final irony

hangs over the ending as Tanya, the cantina owner and Quinlan's only friend other than Menzies, arrives and pronounces his laconic epitaph, "He was some kind of man. What does it matter what you say about people?"

Like most of Welles' films, *Touch of Evil* had many problems in production and in release. It was previewed in 1958 at a length, according to varying sources, of between 105 and 114 minutes. The results of the preview were disappointing to the studio, so they ordered some additional explicatory scenes and some re-editing. As Welles had already left, Universal hired director Harry Keller to supervise the work. The result was a release print running 95 minutes. In 1998, producer Rich Schmidlin supervised the 'restoration' of the movie to a version which ran 111 minutes and was based on extensive notes written by Welles himself.

Still from 'The Big Combo' (1955)
Susan Lowell (Jean Wallace) comforts Diamond. The characters are overtly sexual. Mr Brown lavishes Susan's body with kisses, and treats her like a precious object. She responds to his power with oral sex. Diamond, on the other hand, sleeps with a burlesque dancer; when she is murdered Diamond laments that he put her on and off like a glove. Mr Brown's hitmen Fante and Mingo are obviously gay lovers, although this cannot be stated.

"To realize the power of light and what it can do to the mind of the audience, visualize the following little scene: The room is dark. A strong streak of light sneaks in from the hall under the door. The sound of steps is heard. The shadows of two feet divide the light streak. A brief silence follows. There is suspense in the air. Who is it? What is going to happen? Is he going to ring the bell? Or just insert a key and try to come in? Another heavier shadow appears and blocks the light entirely. A dim hissing sound is heard, and as the shadow leaves, we see in the dim light a paper slip onto the carpet. The steps are heard again... This time they leave. A strong light appears once more and illuminates the note on the floor. We read it as the steps fade out in the distance. 'It is ten o'clock. Please turn off your radio. The Manager.'"

Cinematographer John Alton [18]

Still from 'The Big Combo' (1955)
At the end of the film, with Mr Brown dead, Susan and Diamond wait for the police at the aircraft hangar. This atmospheric shot was the result of cinematographer John Alton's ingenuity. He dressed a studio with the doors, a wheel barrow and some lights, then added a lot of fog.

ABOVE
Still from 'Touch of Evil' (1958)
When Hank Quinlan (Orson Welles) finds some dynamite in Manolo Sanchez's apartment, Ramon Miguel Vargas (Charlton Heston) knows Quinlan is framing the boy. But, however rotten Quinlan's methods, it later transpires that he was right.

RIGHT
On the set of 'Touch of Evil' (1958)
Janet Leigh and director/actor/writer Orson Welles enjoy themselves during the making of the film, despite the fact that Leigh had broken her left arm and Welles had twisted his ankle. Leigh's arm is always covered or hidden in the film, whilst Quinlan's cane helped support Welles for real.

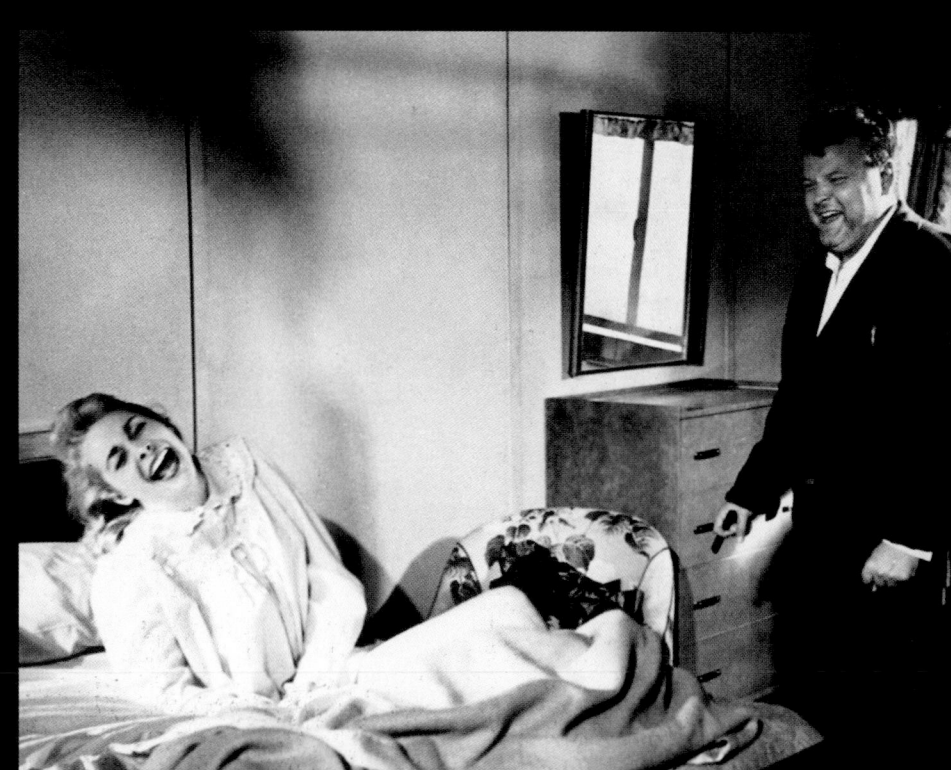

Orson Welles

Orson Welles was born in Kenosha, Wisconsin on 6 May 1915. Among all the directors of noir, Welles has the most prestigious mainstream reputation, based mostly on his landmark 1941 debut film *Citizen Kane*. Welles' roots are in the theatre, as one can see from his emphasis on literary adaptations, sophisticated dialogue and expressionistic staging. He acted in both Ireland and New York in the early 1930s but quickly advanced to the position of writer, producer and director while still acting in his own productions. His first big break was with John Houseman and the New York Federal Theater Project where he staged revolutionary versions of classics like *Macbeth,* set in Haiti, and *Julius Caesar,* set in Fascist Italy. Houseman and Welles ultimately formed their own company called The Mercury Theater and expanded into radio where Welles' became a household name after the infamous 1938 broadcast of *War of the Worlds,* in which the events from H.G. Wells' novel were reported as if they were real, to the actual horror of a significant percentage of his listening audience. Welles traded on the notoriety from *War of the Worlds* and signed a contract with RKO to make a series of films. The first was *Citizen Kane,* loosely based on the life of media magnate William Randolph Hearst. It was a critical success, but like all of Welles' films, marked by one difficulty after another. In this case Hearst tried to prevent the distribution of the movie by buying it out from under Welles and, when RKO refused to sell it, compelled all his newspapers to carry on the attack. Welles continued acting on the radio and in film while directing and writing films in the noir vein like *The Stranger* (1946) and *The Lady from Shanghai* (1948). His love of the classics also continued as he adapted both *Macbeth* (1948) and *Othello* (1952), both memorable for their baroque visual style as well as their troubled production histories. He returned to the realm of noir with *Mr. Arkadin/Confidential Report* (1955) and finally *Touch of Evil*. For the remainder of his career Welles travelled the world, acting extensively while directing films when he could, often in pieces to be put together later. Among the most notable are *The Trial* (1962) and *Chimes at Midnight/Falstaff* (1966). Welles died in Hollywood on 10 October 1985.

ABOVE
Make-Up Test for 'Citizen Kane' (1941)
This is a rare colour make-up shot of Orson
Welles in his office drawing make-up and
costume designs for 'Citizen Kane.'

RIGHT
Still from 'The Magnificent Ambersons' (1942)
At the end of the film, Jack Amberson (Ray

Chronology

1867 to 1900 Novels of Emile Zola, father of naturalism and the 'potboiler' combining crime and sex in such notable works as *La Bête Humaine, L'Assommoir,* and *Thérèse Raquin.*

1900 to 1932 German expressionism: in literature, novelist Hanns Heinz Ewers (*Student of Prague, Alraune,* etc.), screenwriter Carl Mayer (*Das Kabinett des Dr Caligari, Der Letzte Mann,* etc.); in art, Edvard Munch, Käthe Kollwitz, Ernst Kirchner, Max Beckmann, etc.; and in film, Robert Wiene (*Das Kabinett des Dr Caligari*), Fritz Lang (*Metropolis, M*), F.W. Murnau (*Der Letzte Mann*), etc. The movement's emphasis on externalization of emotions and psychology, distortion of reality and symbolism will profoundly influence future noir film-makers.

1912 *The Musketeers of Pig Alley*: early proto-noir short featuring a sordid urban environment and a crime melodrama with angular framing and other stylistic innovations, directed by cinema pioneer D.W. Griffith.

1919 *Broken Blossoms*: Griffith's dark evocation of fin-de-siècle London anticipates elements of the noir style.

1920 to 1940 *Black Mask* magazine, edited by H.L. Mencken and George Jean Nathan, published numerous noirish crime stories by novelists such as Dashiell Hammett and Raymond Chandler.

1920 to 1935 The Ashcan School of Art: graphic works which often dealt with urban settings and events by artists such as George Bellows and William Glackens.

1926 to 1929 Ernest Hemingway's landmark novels *The Sun also Rises* and *A Farewell to Arms* are published, notable for their naturalistic stories and clipped but quasi-poetic dialogue.

1927 to 1928 Josef von Sternberg stylistically anticipates the noir cycle with his silent gangster trilogy, *Underworld, The Dragnet,* and *The Docks of New York.*

1928 The execution of Judd Gray and Ruth Snyder for the 'double indemnity' murder of her husband Albert the previous year, after a sensational trial covered by hundreds of reporters including James M. Cain.

1929 *The Maltese Falcon*: groundbreaking noir novel by Dashiell Hammett is published, shortly followed by *The Glass Key* in 1930. *Menschen am Sonntag*: German documentary featuring the talents of future émigrés and noir film-makers Robert and Curt Siodmak, Edgar G. Ulmer, Billy Wilder and Fred Zinnemann.

1930 to 1939 The Universal Horror cycle with its heavily expressionistic design and lighting, most notably Tod Browning's *Dracula,* Karl Freund's *The Mummy,* Edgar G. Ulmer's *The Black Cat* and James Whale's *Bride of Frankenstein.* Warner Bros. Gangster series with its tales of urban crime and corruption, most notably Howard Hawks' *Scarface,* William Wellman's *Public Enemy,* Mervyn LeRoy's *Little Caesar* and Raoul Walsh's *The Roaring Twenties.* Also the first two adaptations of *The Maltese Falcon* in 1931 and 1936 (as *Satan Met a Lady*).

1930 to 1950 French Poetic Realism: fatalistic brooding films such as Jean Renoir's adaptation of Zola's *La Bête humaine,* Marcel Carné's *Le Jour se lève* and Henri-Georges Clouzot's *Quai des brumes.* During World War, Renoir directs two noir films in Hollywood.

1931 to 1950 Edward Hopper, whose paintings evoked bleak, lonely and often urban landscapes, and other American realist artists succeed the Ashcan school.

1933 to 1941 Scores of writers, composers, artists, and film-makers, many of them of the Jewish faith menaced by the institutionalized anti-Semitism, emigrate from Europe to the United States.

1934 to 1936 *The Postman Always Rings Twice*: sensational crime novel by James M. Cain published, followed two years later by the novella *Double Indemnity.*

1935 to 1945 Arthur Fellig roams the streets of New York City as Weegee, a freelance photographer of the city after dark whose pictures include many grisly crime scenes. His book *The Naked City* (1945) inspires the noir film of that title and his style heavily influences Stanley Kubrick.

1939 *The Big Sleep*: hard-boiled novel by Raymond Chandler published, followed the next year by *Farewell, My Lovely.*

1940 *Stranger on the Third Floor,* starring Peter Lorre and considered by many to be the first film noir.

1941 *The Maltese Falcon*: first noir adaptation of writer Dashiell Hammett's work, starring Humphrey Bogart and the 'official' beginning of the noir movement or classic period.

1941 to 1946 Many of the technical innovations of World War II from better optics and film stocks to use of alloys for lighter equipment are used by the American film industry.

1942 Cornell Woolrich's *Phantom Lady* is published and two years later adapted by Robert Siodmak into a classic film noir. *Street of Chance* adapted from Woolrich's *Black Curtain* is released. Paramount releases adaptations of *The Glass Key* and Graham Greene's *This Gun for Hire* both starring Alan Ladd.

1942 to 1952 Italian Neorealism: beginning with the first adaptation of *The Postman Always Rings Twice, Ossessione,* by Luchino Visconti and stretching through *Roma, città aperta (Rome, Open City), Paisà (Paisan)* and *Ladri di biciclette (The Bicycle Thief)* among others, gave low-budget productions shot on location international respectability.

1943 Production begins on *Double Indemnity*: convergence of the prose talents of Raymond Chandler and James M. Cain with those of director Billy Wilder and Paramount's best noir craftsmen in one of the earliest A-budget studio noirs.

1944 Chandler's *Farewell My Lovely* is adapted by RKO as *Murder, My Sweet,* and Twentieth Century-Fox releases *Laura.*

1945 *Detour*: Edgar G. Ulmer's Z-budget noir, steeped in German Expressionism. Fritz Lang's studies of middle-aged obsession, *The Woman in the Window* and *Scarlet Street,* are released.

1946 *The Postman Always Rings Twice*: sensual adaptation of Cain's classic noir novel. *Dark Passage*: David Goodis' masochistic noir novel

published and later adapted into a film with Humphrey Bogart (released 1947).
Gilda: classic femme fatale noir movie, starring Rita Hayworth as the vamp.
The Big Sleep: directed by Howard Hawks, based on the novel by Chandler and starring noir icon Humphrey Bogart as private eye Marlowe.
The Killers: based on the Nick Adams short stories by Ernest Hemingway, directed by Robert Siodmak.
Post-war French reviewers Nino Frank and Jean-Pierre Chartier discover a spate of American pictures made in a particular style, which they dub 'noir,' the epithet for a series of hard-boiled novels.

1947 Producer Mark Hellinger first teams with director Jules Dassin for *Brute Force*. *Out of the Past* is released by RKO.
Actor/Director Robert Montgomery follows his all-subjective-camera adaptation of Chandler's *Lady in the Lake* with the more traditionally staged *Ride the Pink Horse* in the same year.

1947 to 1955 The House Un-American Activities Committee (HUAC) hearings on Hollywood, which resulted in the black- and gray-listing of many writers and directors of the noir movement including Dalton Trumbo, Albert Maltz, Edward Dmytryk, Abraham Polonsky and Joseph Losey.

1948 *T-Men*: from noir stylists Anthony Mann and John Alton, one of the first documentary style noirs. Also released, the Dassin/Hellinger *The Naked City*.

1949 *He Walked by Night*: directed by Mann (uncredited) and Alfred Werker, a docu-noir about a serial killer which featured the first appearance of Jack Webb as a police detective who became Joe Friday, hero of the docu-noir series *Dragnet* on radio (1949–1956) drama and television (1951–1959 and 1967–1970).
Ophüls' stylish duo, *Caught* and *The Reckless Moment* are released, as well as Siodmak's *Criss Cross* and Nicholas Ray's *Knock on any Door*.

1950 The peak of noir with over 30 studio productions released including *The Asphalt Jungle* (MGM), *The File on Thelma Jordon* (Paramount) *In a Lonely Place* (Columbia), *Kiss Tomorrow Goodbye* (Warner Bros.), *Night and the City* (Twentieth Century-Fox), *The Sleeping City* (Universal) and *Where Danger Lives* (RKO).
United Artists releases two independent classics: *Gun Crazy* Lewis' landmark rendering of the 'couple on the run' and *D.O.A.*'s 'dead man walking.'

1951 Noir with a social conscience: *The Big Carnival* (aka *Ace in the Hole*) from Wilder, *The Big Night* from Joseph Losey, and *The Enforcer* from Raoul Walsh.

1952 Ray's violent cop study *On Dangerous Ground* and actor/director Ray Milland's quirky noir without dialogue *The Thief*.

1953 Sex and violence: Preminger's *Angel Face*; Lang's *The Big Heat* and *Blue Gardenia*; Samuel Fuller's *Pick-up on South Street*.

1954 *Human Desire*: directed by Fritz Lang, classic adaptation of Zola's *La Bête humaine*. Off-beat B's: Andre de Toth's *Crime Wave* and Don Siegel's *Private Hell 36*.

1955 French critics Raymond Borde and Etienne Chaumeton publish *Panorama du film noir américain*, the first book-length study of film noir.
Kiss Me Deadly, the nihilistic reworking of the detective noir drama. Also Lewis' *The Big Combo*, Stanley Kubrick's debut with *Killer's Kiss* and Welles' *Mr. Arkadin*.

1956 Declining returns: *The Killing*, Stanley Kubrick's time-distorted caper film, Hitchcock's *The Wrong Man*, and Fritz Lang's twist of that theme, *Beyond a Reasonable Doubt*.

1957 The noir cycle announces *Sweet Smell of Success*, "a cookie filled with arsenic," and its prognosis is poor.

1958 *The Lineup*, Siegel's blend of noir themes in a documentary style, and *Touch of Evil*, Welles' last studio picture and what many will consider the swansong of the classic noir cycle.

1959 to 1962 A few stragglers from *Odds Against Tomorrow* to *Cape Fear*.

1967 *Point Blank*: transitional picture by British director John Boorman with a noir protagonist in post-noir Los Angeles.

1970 English critic Raymond Durgnat's article 'Family Tree of Film Noir' is published in *Cinema*.

1971 Paul Schrader's 'notes on film noir' accompany a retrospective at Filmex (the Los Angeles Film Exposition). They are reprinted the following spring as an article in *Film Comment*.

1972 *Hickey & Boggs*: screenwriter Walter Hill's homage to the classic period features two old school PIs, who are self-conscious of their own anachronism ("There's nothing left to this profession. It's all over; it's not about anything."), and is arguably the first neo-noir.

1974 *Chinatown*: screenwriter Robert Towne and director Roman Polanski's period detective drama set in a pre-noir 1930s Los Angeles and usually cited as the first neo-noir. Also released: *The Conversation* by Francis Ford Coppola.

1976 Martin Scorsese directs *Taxi Driver* from Paul Schrader's noir-inspired script.

1977 *The Driver*: Walter Hill's heavily stylized neo-noir.

1981 to present *Body Heat*: written and directed by Lawrence Kasdan, this feature firmly establishes neo-noir as a genre that continues to this day as a self-conscious reflection on the classic period by a new generation of film-makers. Also released this year are Bob Rafelson's remake of *The Postman Always Rings Twice* and Michael Mann's *Thief*.

ABOVE
On the set of 'Gilda' (1946)
Rita Hayworth is helped into or out of her dress.

OPPOSITE TOP
Still from 'M' (1931)
Hans Beckert (Peter Lorre) is marked with the letter M for Murderer. This mark will allow the criminals to hunt him down and put him on trial.

OPPOSITE BOTTOM
Still from 'La Bête humaine' (1938)
Jacques Lantier (Jean Gabin) kills Séverine (Simone Simon) during one of his fits.

Filmography

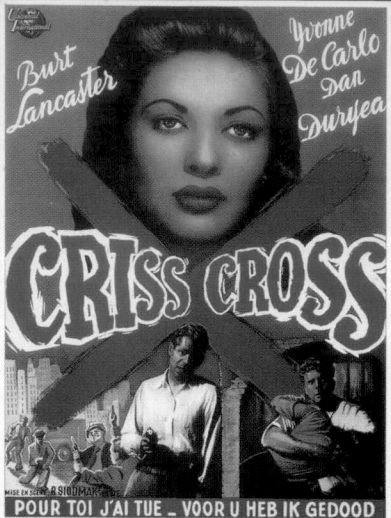

Criss Cross (1949)

Crew: *Director* Robert Siodmak, *Producer* Michel Kraik, *Screenplay* Daniel Fuchs, *Novel* Don Tracy, *Director of Photography* Franz Planer, *Art Director* Bernard Herzbrun & Boris Leven, *Costumes* Yvonne Wood, *Music* Miklós Rózsa, *Editor* Ted J. Kent, *Distributor* Universal-International, Released 12 January 1949, 88 minutes.
Cast: Burt Lancaster (Steve Thompson/Narrator), Yvonne De Carlo (Anna Dundee), Dan Duryea (Slim Dundee), Stephen McNally (Detective Lt. Pete Ramirez), Tom Pedi (Vincent), Percy Helton (Frank), Richard Long (Slade Thompson), Alan

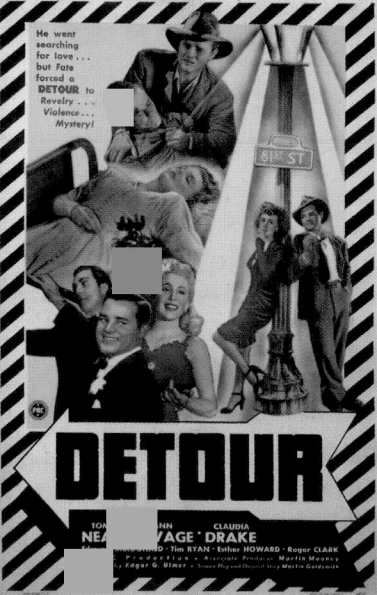

Napier (Finchley), Griff Barnett (Pop), Meg Randall (Helen), Joan Miller (Drunk at Roundup Bar), Edna Holland (Mrs. Thompson), Esy Morales (Orchestra leader), John Doucette (Walt), Marc Krah (Mort), James O'Rear (Waxie), John Miller (Midget).

Detour (1945)

Crew: *Director* Edgar G. Ulmer, *Producer* Leon Fromkess, *Screenplay* Martin Goldsmith and Martin Mooney [uncredited], *Novel* Martin Goldsmith, *Director of Photography* Benjamin H. Kline, *Art Director* Edward C. Jewell, *Costumes* Mona Barry, *Music* Leo Erdody, *Editor* George McGuire, *Distributor* PRC, Released 30 November 1945, 68 minutes.
Cast: Tom Neal (Al Roberts), Ann Savage (Vera), Claudia Drake (Sue), Edmund MacDonald (Haskell), Tim Ryan (Diner Owner), Esther Howard (Waitress), Roger Clark (Cop), Pat Gleason (Joe the Trucker), Don Brodie (Used-car Salesman), Eddie Hall (Tony the car-lot Mechanic), Harry Strang (Border Patrolman).

Double Indemnity (1944)

Crew: *Director* Billy Wilder, *Producer* Joseph Sistrom [uncredited], *Screenplay* Billy Wilder & Raymond Chandler, *Novella* James M. Cain, *Director of Photography* John F. Seitz, *Art Directors* Hans Dreier & Hal Pereira, *Costumes* Edith Head, *Music* Miklós Rózsa with adaptations from César Franck's 'D Minor Symphony', *Editor* Doane Harrison, *Distributor* Paramount, Released 7 September 1944, 106 minutes.
Cast: Fred MacMurray (Walter Neff), Barbara Stanwyck (Phyllis Dietrichson), Edward G.

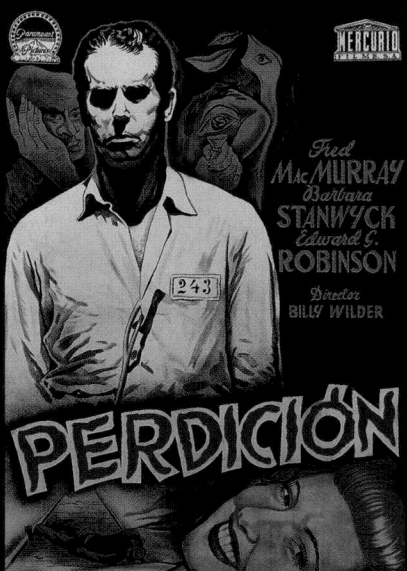

Robinson (Barton Keyes), Porter Hall (Mr. Jackson), Jean Heather (Lola Dietrichson), Tom Powers (Mr. Dietrichson), Byron Barr (Nino Zachetti), Richard Gaines (Edward S. Norton), Fortunio Bonanova (Sam Gorlopis), John Philliber (Joe Peters).

Gun Crazy (1950)

Crew: *Director* Joseph H. Lewis, *Producers* Maurice King & Frank King [King Brothers Productions/Pioneer Pictures], *Screenplay* Dalton Trumbo [uncredited], Mackinlay Kantor, 'Millard Kaufman' [front for Trumbo], *Story* Mackinlay Kantor, *Director of Photography* Russell Harlan, *Art Director* Gordon Wiles, *Costumes* Norma [Koch], *Music* Victor Young, *Song Lyrics* Ned Washington, *Editor* Harry Gerstad, *Distributor* United Artists, Released as *Deadly is the Female*, 26 January 1950 and as *Gun Crazy*, 24 August 1950, 87 minutes.
Cast: Peggy Cummins (Annie Laurie Starr), John Dall (Bart Tare), Berry Kroeger (Packett), Morris Carnovsky (Judge Willoughby), Anabel Shaw (Ruby Tare), Harry Lewis (Clyde Boston), Nedrick Young (Dave Allister), Trevor Bardette (Sheriff Boston), Mickey Little (Bart Tare, Age 7), Rusty Tamblyn (Bart Tare, Age 14), Paul Frison (Clyde Boston, Age 14), David Bair (Dave Allister, Age 14), Stanley Prager (Bluey-Bluey), Virginia Farmer (Miss Wynn), Anne O'Neal (Miss Sifert), Frances Irwin (Danceland Singer), Don Beddoe (Man from Chicago), Robert Osterloh (Hampton Policeman), Shimen Ruskin (Taxi Driver), Harry Hayden (Mr. Mallenberg), Ray Teal (Border Patrolman).

In a Lonely Place (1950)

Crew: *Director* Nicholas Ray, *Producer* Robert Lord (Santana Productions), *Screenplay* Andrew Solt, Edmund H. North (adaptation), *Novel* Dorothy B. Hughes, *Director of Photography* Burnett Guffey, *Art Director* Robert Peterson, *Costumes* Jean Louis, *Music* George Antheil, *Editor* Viola Lawrence, *Distributor* Columbia, Released 17 May 1950, 94 minutes.
Cast: Humphrey Bogart (Dixon Steele), Gloria Grahame (Laurel Gray), Frank Lovejoy (Brub

Nicolai), Carl Benton Reid (Lochner), Art Smith Mel Lippman), Jeff Donnell (Sylvia Nicolai), Martha Stewart (Mildred Atkinson), Robert Warwick (Charlie Waterman), Morris Ankrum Lloyd Barnes), William Ching (Ted Barton), Steven Geray (Paul), Hadda Brooks (Singer), Alice Talton Frances), [...] Reynolds (Henry Kessler), Ruth Warren (E[...]th Gillette (Martha), Guy Beach Swan), Lewis Howard (Junior).

Kiss Me Deadly (1955)

Crew: *Director/Producer* Robert Aldrich Parklane Productions], *Executive Producer* Victor Seville, *Screenplay* A.I. Bezzerides, *Novel* Mickey Spillane, *Director of Photography* Ernest Laszlo, *Art Director* William Glasgow, *Music* Frank DeVol, *Song* 'Rather Have the Blues' lyrics and music Frank DeVol sung by Nat 'King' Cole, *Editor* Michael Luciano, *Distributor* United Artists, Released 18 May 1955, 105 minutes.
Cast: Ralph Meeker (Mike Hammer), Albert Dekker (Dr Soberin), Paul Stewart (Carl Evello),

(Gabrielle/Lily Carver), Wesley Addy (Pat Murphy), Juano Hernandez (Eddie Yeager), Nick Dennis (Nick), Cloris Leachman (Christina), Marian Carr (Friday), Jack Lambert (Sugar), Jack Elam (Charlie Max), Jerry Zinneman (Sammy), Percy Helton (Morgue Attendant), Fortunio Bonanova (Carmen Trivago), Silvio Minciotti (Old Mover), Leigh Snowden (Girl at Pool), Madi Comfort (Singer), Art Loggins (Bartender), Robert Cornthwaite, James Seay (FBI Men), Mara McAfee (Nurse), James McCallian ('Super'), Jesslyn Fax (Mrs. 'Super'), Mort Marshall (Ray Diker), Strother Martin (Truck Driver), Marjorie Bennett (Manager), Robert Sherman (Gas Station Man), Keith McConnell (Athletic Club Clerk).

Out of the Past (1947)

Crew: *Director* Jacques Tourneur, *Executive Producer* Robert Sparks, *Producer* Warren Duff, *Screenplay* Geoffrey Homes [pseudonym for Daniel Mainwaring], Frank Fenton [uncredited], James M. Cain [uncredited], *Novel Build My Gallows High* Geoffrey Homes, *Director of Photography* Nicholas Musuraca, *Art Directors* Albert S. D'Agostino & Jack Okey, *Costumes* Edward Stevenson, *Music* Roy Webb, *Editor* Samuel E. Beetley, *Distributor* RKO, Released 25 November 1947, 96 minutes.
Cast: Robert Mitchum (Jeff Bailey/Markham), Jane Greer (Kathie Moffat), Kirk Douglas (Whit Sterling), Rhonda Fleming (Meta Carson), Richard Webb (Jim), Steve Brodie (Fisher), Virginia Huston (Ann), Paul Valentine (Joe), Dickie Moore (Boy), Ken Niles (Eels the Lawyer).

The Reckless Moment (1949)

Crew: *Director* Max Ophüls, *Producer* Walter Wanger, *Screenplay* Robert W[...]oderberg & Henry Garson, *Adaptation* Robert E. Kent & Mel Dinelli, *Novel The Blank Wall* Elisabeth Sanxay Holding, *Director of Photography* Burnett Guffey, *Art Director* Cary Odell, *Costumes* Jean Louis, *Music* Hans Salter, *Editor* Gene Havlick, *Distributor* Columbia, Released 29 December 1949, 81 minutes.
Cast: James Mason (Martin Donnelly), Joan

Left poster text:

GAUMONT *présente* UNE PRODUCTION EDWARD SMALL *de* EAGLE-LION FILMS Inc.

DENNIS O'KEEFE

DANS

LA BRIGADE DU SUICIDE
(T'MEN)

avec

MARY MEADE . ALFRED RYDER . WALLY FORD . JUNE LOCKHART
et CHARLES McGRAW

Produit par AUBREY SCHENCK - Réalisation de ANTHONY MANN - Scénario de JOHN C. HIGGINS
D'après une nouvelle de VIRGINIA KELLOGG
Distribuée par GAUMONT· 40, Champs-Elysées PARIS.

(Moxie), Jane Randolph (Diana), Art Smith (Chief Gregg), Herbert Heyes (Chief Carson), Jack Overman (Brownie), John Wengraf (Shiv), Jim Bannon (Lindsay), William Malten (Miller), Reed Hadley (Narrator), Vivian Austin (Genevieve), Anton Kosta (Vantucci), Tito Vuolo (Pasquale), James Seay (Hardy), John Newland (Jackson Lee), Lyle Latell (Isgreg), Robert Williams (Detective Captain).

Touch of Evil (1958)

Crew: *Director/Screenplay* Orson Welles, *Producer* Albert Zugsmith [Universal], *Novel Badge of Evil* Whit Masterson, *Director of Photography* Russell Metty, *Art Directors* Alexander Golitzen & Robert Clatworthy, *Costumes* Bill Thomas, *Music* Henry Mancini, *Editors* Virgil M. Vogel & Aaron Stell, *Distributor* Universal-International, Released 21 May 1958, 95 minutes, 111 minutes [restored version].

Cast: Charlton Heston (Mike Vargas), Janet Leigh (Susan Vargas), Orson Welles (Hank Quinlan), Joseph Calleia (Pete Menzies), Akim Tamiroff (Uncle Joe Grandi), Joanna Moore (Marcia Linnekar), Marlene Dietrich (Tanya), Ray Collins (D.A. Adair), Dennis Weaver (Motel Manager), Victor Millan (Manolo Sanchez), Valentin de Vargas (Pancho), Mort Mills (Schwartz), Mercedes McCambridge (Hoodlum), Zsa Zsa Gabor (Nightclub Owner), Keenan Wynn (Man), Harry Shannon (Chief Gould), Joseph Cotten (Detective), Phil Harvey (Blaine), Michael Sargent (Pretty Boy).

Bennett (Lucia Harper), Geraldine Brooks (Beatrice Harper), Henry O'Neill (Mr. Harper), Shepperd Strudwick (Ted Darby), David Bair (David Harper), Roy Roberts (Nagle), Frances Williams (Sybil), Paul E. Burns (Desk Clerk), Danny Jackson (Drummer), Claire Carleton (Blonde), Billy Snyder (Gambler), Peter Brocco (Bartender), Karl 'Killer' Davis (Wrestler), Virginia Hunter (Girl), Joe Palma (Card Player), Penny O'Connor (Liza), Bruce Gilbert Norman (Dennis), Sharon Monaghan (Bridget), Bobby Hyatt (M...), Ann Shoemaker (Mrs. Feller), Everett Glass (Drug Clerk), Buddy Gorman (Magazine Clerk), Louis Mason (Mike), Charles Marsh (Newsman), Norman Leavitt, Harry Harvey (Postal Clerks), Body Davis (Tall Man), Pat Barton (Receptionist), John Butler (Pawnbroker), Kathryn Card (Mrs. Loring), Pat O'Malley (Bank Guard), Charles Evans (Bank Official), Jessie Arnold (Old Lady).

T-Men (1948)

Crew: *Director* Anthony Mann, *Executive Producer* Edward Small [Reliance Pictures], *Producer* Aubrey Schenck, *Writer* John C. Higgins, *Story* Virginia Kellogg, *Based* upon the files of the U.S. Treasury Department, *Director of Photography* John Alton, *Art Director* Edward C. Jewell, *Costumes* Frances Ehren, *Music* Paul Sawtell, *Editor* Fred Allen, *Distributor* Eagle-Lion, Released 22 January 1948, 92 minutes.

Cast: Dennis O'Keefe (Dennis O'Brien/Hannigan), Alfred Ryder (Tony Genaro/Galvani), Mary Meade (Evangeline), Wallace Ford (Schemer), June Lockhart (Genaro's wife), Charles McGraw

Bibliography

Books by Alain Silver and James Ursini

— *Film Noir: An Encyclopedic Reference to the American Style*, Third Edition, co-edited with Elizabeth Ward, Robert Porfirio and Carl Macek. New York: Overlook Press, 1992. Details on 300 titles with several appendices covering neo-noir, other books on noir and cross-listing titles by studio, release year and key film-makers.
— *Film Noir Reader.* New York: Limelight Editions, 1996. All the seminal essays in one volume plus eight case studies and new articles on the fugitive couple, femme fatales and neo-noir.
— *Film Noir Reader 2.* New York: Limelight Editions, 1999. More seminal pieces plus eight more case studies by Robin Word, Robert Porfirio and Elizabeth Ward and seven new essays including British Noir and Noir 101.
— *Film Noir Reader 3: Interviews with Filmmakers of the Classic Noir Period,* edited with Robert Porfirio. New York: Limelight Editions, 2002. Previously unpublished interviews about noir with directors such as Edward Dmytryk, Billy Wilder, Joseph H. Lewis, Fritz Lang and Otto Preminger, writer Daniel Mainwaring, cinematographers John F. Seitz and James Wong Howe, composer Miklós Rózsa and actresses Claire Trevor and Lizabeth Scott.
— *Film Noir Reader 4: The Crucial Films and Themes.* New York: Limelight Editions, 2004. New essays on the prototype films and the main themes of noir by Robert Porfirio, J.P. Telotte, R. Barton Palmer and Robin Wood.
— *The Noir Style.* New York: Overlook Press, 1999. An in-depth analysis of the visual style of noir with numerous duo-tone illustrations organized along the themes of noir such as 'Night and the City', 'Deadly is the Female' and 'The Dark Mirror.'

Books

— Alloway, Lawrence: *Violent America: The Movies, 1946-1964.* New York: Museum of Modern Art, 1971.
— Borde, Raymond & Chaumeton, Etienne: *Panorama du film noir américain, 1941-1953.* San Francisco: City Lights Books, 2002, translated by Paul Hammond.
— Cameron, Ian (Ed.): *The Book of Film Noir.* New York: Continuum, 1993.
— Christopher, Nicholas: *Somewhere in the Night.* New York: Free Press, 1997.
— Copjec, Joan (Ed.): *Shades of Noir: A Reader.* London; New York: Verso, 1993.
— Dumont, Hervé: *Robert Siodmak: Le maître du film noir.* Lausanne: Editions L'Age d'Homme, 1981.
— Duncan, Paul: *Film Noir: Films of Trust and Betrayal.* London: Pocket Essentials, 2001.
— Gifford, Barry: *The Devil Thumbs a Ride, and Other Unforgettable Films.* New York: Grove Press, 1988.
— Gorman, Ed, Server, Lee & Greenberg, Martin (Eds.): *The Big Book of Noir.* New York: Carroll & Graf, 1998.
— Kaplan, E. Ann (ed.): *Women in Film Noir.* London: BFI Publishing, 1998 (Revised Edition).
— Karimi, Amir Massoud: *Toward a Definition of the American Film Noir (1941-1949).* New York: Arno Press, 1976.
— Krutnik, Frank: *In a Lonely Street: Film Noir, Genre, Masculinity.* New York: Routledge, 1991.
— McArthur, Colin: *Underworld U.S.A.* New York: Viking Press, 1972.
— Muller, Eddie: *The Art of Film Noir.* Woodstock: Overlook Press, 2002.
— Muller, Eddie: *Dark City, The Lost World of Film Noir.* New York: St. Martin's Press, 1998.
— Muller, Eddie: *Dark City Dames.* New York: Regan Books, 2001.
— Naremore, James: *More Than Night: Film Noir in its Contexts.* Berkeley: University of California Press, 1998.
— Oliver, Kelly & Benigno Trigo: *Noir Anxiety.* Minneapolis: University of Minnesota Press, 2003.
— Ottoson, Robert: *A Reference Guide to the American Film Noir, 1940-1958.* Metuchen, N.J.: Scarecrow Press, 1981.

— Palmer, R. Barton: *Hollywood's Dark Cinema: the American Film Noir.* New York: Twayne Publishers, 1994.
— Palmer, R. Barton (Ed.): *Perspectives on Film Noir.* New York: G.K. Hall, 1996.
— Phillips, Gene D.: *Creatures of Darkness: Raymond Chandler, Detective Fiction, and Film Noir.* Lexington, Kentucky: University of Kentucky Press, 2000.
— Porfirio, Robert: *The Dark Age of American Film: A Study of American Film Noir (1940-1960).* Unpublished Doctoral Dissertation, Yale University, 1979.
— Richardson, Carl: *Autopsy: An Element of Realism in Film Noir.* Metuchen, N.J.: Scarecrow Press, 1992.
— Rosow, Eugene: *Born to Lose: The Gangster Film in America.* New York: Oxford University Press, 1978.
— Selby, Spencer: *Dark City: The Film Noir.* Jefferson, N.C.: McFarland, 1984.
— Shadoian, Jack: *Dreams and Dead Ends: The American Gangster/Crime Film.* Cambridge, Massachusetts: MIT Press, 1977.
— Telotte, J.P.: *Voices in the Dark: The Narrative Patterns of Film Noir.* Urbana, Illinois: University of Illinois Press, 1989.
— Thompson, Peggy & Usukawa, Saeko: *Hard-Boiled: Great Lines from Classic Noir Films.* San Francisco: Chronicle Books, 1995.

Articles

— Biesen, Sheri Chinen: 'Bogart, Bacall, Howard Hawks and Wartime Film Noir at Warner Bros.: *To Have and Have Not* and *The Big Sleep.' Popular Culture Review,* January, 2002.
— Biesen, Sheri Chinen: 'Censorship, Film Noir, and *Double Indemnity* (1944).' *Film & History,* 1995 (1-2).
— Capp, Rose: 'B-girls, dykes and doubles: *Kiss Me Deadly* and the legacy of 'late noir.'' *Screening the Past,* July, 2000.
— Gallagher, Brian: '"I Love You Too": Sexual Warfare & Homoeroticism in Billy Wilder's *Double Indemnity.' Literature/Film Quarterly,* 1987 (15/4).
— Garrett, Greg: 'The Many Faces of *Mildred Pierce*: A Case Study of Adaptation and the Studio System.' *Literature/Film Quarterly,* 1995 (23/4).
— Hill, R.F.: 'Remembrance, Communication and *Kiss Me Deadly.' Literature-Film Quarterly,* 1995 (23/2).
— Jensen, Paul: 'The Writer: Raymond Chandler and the World You Live In.' *Film Comment,* November/December, 1974.
— Krohn, Bill: '*Touch of Evil,* épitaphe du film noir.' *Cahiers du cinéma,* January, 1994.
— Lang, Robert: 'Looking for the 'Great Whatzit': *Kiss Me Deadly* and Film Noir.' *Cinema Journal,* Spring, 1988.
— Leibman, Nina C.: 'Piercing the Truth: Mildred and Patriarchy.' *Literature in Performance,* November, 1988.
— Orr, Christopher: 'Cain, naturalism and noir.' *Film Criticism,* Fall, 2000.
— Palmer, James W.: '*In a Lonely Place*: Paranoia in the Dream Factory.' *Literature/Film Quarterly,* 1985 (13/3).
— Polan, Dana: 'Film Noir.' *Journal of Film and Video,* Spring, 1985.
— Schwager, J.: 'The Past Rewritten: How Screenwriters Re-wrote the Film Noir Classic *Out of the Past.' Film Comment,* January/February, 1991.
— Stubbs, John: 'The Evolution of Orson Welles' *Touch of Evil* from Novel to Film.' *Cinema Journal,* Winter, 1985.
— Thomson, David: 'A Cottage at Palos Verdes (*Criss Cross*).' *Film Comment,* May-June, 1990.

Websites

— www.lib.berkeley.edu/MRC/Noirbib.html
— www.eskimo.com/~noir/
— www.filmnoirreader.com
— www.noirstyle.com
— www.imdb.com

Notes

1. Bogdanovich, Peter: *Who the Devil Made it.* New York: Knopf, 1997. Pgs. 251-252.
2. Porfirio, Robert & Silver, Alain & Ursini, James (Eds.): *Film Noir Reader 3: Interviews with Filmmakers of the Classic Noir Period.* New York: Limelight Editions, 2002. Pg. 205.
3. See note 2. Pg. 107.
4. See note 2. Pg. 101.
5. See note 1. Pg. 565.
6. See note 2. Pgs. 150/155.
7. Server, Lee: *Robert Mitchum.* New York: St. Martin's Press, 2001. Pg. 118.
8. Clark, Ronald W.: *Einstein: The Life and Times..* New York: Avon, 1999. Pg. 422.
9. See note 2. Pg. 237.
10. Missiaen, IJean-Claude & Brion, Patrick & Eyquem, Olivier: *Cahiers du Cinema in English.* May 1967. Pg. 46.
11. Lo Duca, Giuseppe: *L'Erotisme au cinéma* (supplement). Montreuil: Édilu, 1968. Pg. 44.
12. See note 2. Pg. 71.
13. Speaking in documentary *I'm a Stranger Here Myself.*
14. Willamen, Paul (Ed.): *Ophüls.* London: BFI, 1958. Pg. 31.
15. Gorman, Ed, Server, Lee & Greenberg, Martin (Eds.): *The Big Book of Noir.* New York: Carroll & Graf, 1998. Pg. 121.
16. Higham, Charles: *The Celluloid Muse.* Chicago: Henry Regnery, 1969. Pgs. 30-31.
17. Silver, Alain: 'Mr. Film Noir Stays at the Table.' *Film Comment,* Spring 1972. Pg. 17.
18. Alton, John: *Painting with Light.* New York: MacMillan, 1949. Pg. 56.

Acknowledgements

We have been writing about film noir for over twenty-five years and, during that time, many fellow writers, film-makers and fans have sent us comments, criticisms and corrections. It would be impossible to acknowledge them all, but we must single out our most frequent collaborators on past work: Elizabeth Ward, whose determination and effort held together the initial compilation of *Film Noir: An Encyclopedic Reference*; Robert Porfirio, not just for his substantial contribution to that volume but also for adding to the five others that followed and to *The Reckless Moment* herein; and Linda Brookover, whose work on the original 'What is This Thing Called Noir?' is reflected in the essays on *Gun Crazy* and *Criss Cross*.

Specific Permissions

Kiss Me Deadly is adapted from 'KISS ME DEADLY: Evidence of a Style' published in *Film Comment,* Volume 11, number 2 (March-April, 1975) copyright © 1975 by Alain Silver and is reprinted by permission. *Gun Crazy* and *Criss Cross* are adapted from 'Mad Love' in *UCLA Film Screening Cooperative Program Notes,* May, 1970 copyright © 1970 by Alain Silver and 'What is This Thing Called Noir' in *Film Noir Reader,* New York: Limelight Editions, copyright © 1995 by Linda Brookover and Alain Silver and is reprinted by permission. *The Reckless Moment* is adapted from 'The Ophüls Cycle' in *UCLA Film Screening Cooperative Program Notes,* October, 1969 copyright © 1969 by Alain Silver.

PAGE 192

Still from 'The Third Man' (1949)

Pulp writer Holly Martins (Joseph Cotten) waits for Anna Schmidt (Alida Valli) after the funeral of his friend and her lover Harry Lime. In this famous ending, Anna walks straight past Holly.